THE LIMPLEY STOKE VALL

*Cover: View across the Limpley Stoke Valley with autumnal colours and
the River Avon swollen and reddened by seasonal rains.*

Sun filtering through trees in Murhill Lane

WEST COUNTRY LANDSCAPES

The Limpley Stoke Valley

Margaret Wilson

EX LIBRIS PRESS

First published in 1994 by
EX LIBRIS PRESS
1 The Shambles
Bradford on Avon
Wiltshire

Typeset in 10 point Palatino
Design and typesetting by Ex Libris Press

Cover printed by Shires Press, Trowbridge
Printed in Britian by
Cromwell Press, Broughton Gifford, Wiltshire

ISBN 0 948578 58 0

To my sons.

The Council for the Protection of Rural England

CPRE is one of the country's leading environmental organisations – it is the only independent organisation concerned with the care and improvement of the whole of England's countryside, not simply particular features or elements in it.
CPRE's methods involve careful research, constructive ideas, reasoned argument and a knowledge of how to get things done.
Our business is effective lobbying and real influence.
Funded almost entirely by supporters' donations and legacies, CPRE works for a beautiful and living countryside.
Membership is open to all.
CPRE needs many more members if we are to win better environmental policies for the future. Details of membership are available from CPRE by contacting the following:

CPRE, Warwick House, 25 Buckingham Palace Road,
London, SW1W 0PP   Tel: 071 976 6433

Contents

Series Introduction

The present series, which it is intended should grow into a list of around fifteen titles, deals with significant and identifiable landscapes of the south-western counties. These contain two National Parks – Exmoor and Dartmoor – and several Areas of Outstanding Natural Beauty.

Our preference is for areas of the West Country which are perhaps less well documented than the National Parks, and for books which offer a complete picture of a particular landscape. We favour, too, an author who is sufficiently well acquainted with his or her chosen landscape to present his story in the round and with an ease in the telling which belies his depth of knowledge. Authors for West Country Landscapes have been chosen with this in mind.

The plan of each book is quite simple: the subject's underlying geology is the starting point. From this basis we are led to an understanding of that landscape's topography, of its flora and fauna and of the particular pattern of human settlement to which it gives rise – natural history followed by human history, in other words. Then we may look more closely at people and traditions, and at the interaction between individuals and the landscape – perhaps as expressed in literature and folklore. Throughout each account, there is constant reference to what may be seen on the ground today.

West Country landscapes vary greatly – this is part of their great appeal. Likewise authors vary in their enthusiasms and areas of expertise. All these factors have a bearing on the books which we publish in the West Country Landscapes series. The books are substantial but succinct, well rounded but readable accounts of noteworthy pockets of the West Country, each with its particular characteristics and each penned by individually minded authors.

We are pleased to be associated with the CPRE in the production of the West Country Landscapes series. Any comments and suggestions from readers will be welcomed by the publishers.

Roger Jones, Editor

About the Author

Margaret Wilson has followed a varied career, some of it in North America where she worked for the British Travel Authority before becoming a medical assistant to her husband, first in London, then Seattle. She and her husband took advantage of the spectacular scenery in the Pacific North West, hiking some of the thousands of miles of forest and mountain trails. Margaret admits to following a desire always to live in beautiful places and, on returning to England twenty years ago, moved into a house on the south-facing slopes of the Limpley Stoke Valley. The view, and an increasing awareness of the historical importance of the Valley, inspired her to write this book. It follows her *Tours to Historic Parish Churches near Bath* and *A Touring Guide to Wiltshire Villages* which are illustrated by local artist, Juliet Greaves. In this book Margaret's latent ambition to be a photographer has been given some freedom, while Juliet contributes some of her attractive line drawings.

Acknowledgements

To the many people with local knowledge, especially the Bathford Local History Society and Freshford and District Local History Society, who have been an invaluable source of information. I should particularly like to thank Dr. Alan Dodge, Dr. John Williams, Mr. Godfrey F. Laurence, Mrs. Dody Nicholls, Professor W.H. Dowdeswell and Mrs. Leslie Marshman and the staff in the Archaeological Section of the Library and Museum Service in Trowbridge. Thanks also to Bradford on Avon Library and Museum, Bath Reference Library, Avon Wildlife Trust, English Nature and the P.R. Department of Wessex Water. Special thanks to Simon Tutty in Medical Illustration at Bath's Royal United Hospital for help with the photography, Mr. W. Burraston, Mr. Mervyn Halbrook and Mr. John Willett for contributing old photographs, Juliet Greaves and Dick Ellingham for illustrations, and Devizes Archaeological Museum for permission to adapt photos for line drawings. Thanks to Lady Susan Marshall and Mr. John Harrop for script-reading and my family for help and encouragement.

Note: Throughout the text the abbreviation VHCW has been used to refer to the *Victoria History of the County of Wiltshire.*

Introduction

In the valley of the Bristol Avon, between the Wiltshire town of Bradford on Avon and the City of Bath, the river flows through four miles of unsurpassed English scenery. Here is a gentle landscape, a slice of English countryside which has been sculpted and gilded, shaped to please the eye and is perfect in its composition. This land of riverside meadows and wooded heights, villages and hamlets is known as the Limpley Stoke Valley.

The extraordinary dearth of activity in this century bears no resemblance to the previous four thousand years in the valley and its surroundings. In our present day, except for sheep and cattle and a few crops, the fields are empty and silent, the wooded slopes the same but for occasional tree felling. The numerous woollen mills on the Avon and its tributaries have closed down. The productive stone quarries, their maze of tunnels running deep into the hillsides, are, for the most part, derelict. Only the eighteenth century canal and its towpath, revived for the population's leisure time, shows much sign of life. Trains are an infrequent but often enjoyable addition to the scene and even the car has little impact, at present, on the prevailing calm.

Yet in the past the valley resounded to scarcely imaginable sights and sounds. Thousands of Iron Age folk beavered away building their massive earthworks at three separate fortified camps above the valley. The sounds of axes, choppers and saws on wood have echoed through the surrounding forests from the time of the Bronze Age until the encroaching woodland was finally tamed. Agriculture involved the labours of hundreds of people at one time. The final stages of the great fortification known as Wansdyke stopped short of the valley, but how many muscular men were needed to throw up a great earthwork that would repel the armies from the north?

With a few exceptions, such as the existing sawmill and papermill near Bathford, there is little industry. In the past, the stone quarries, the trolleyways that descended from the quarries to build the Kennet and Avon Canal, the construction of the railway, the coal canal, bridges, aqueducts and local housing all required the labours of a great number of people. Where once a cacophony of sound resounded down the valley – the ring of the anvil, the sound of the saw and the grunts of the labouring serfs – we have the chugging of the newly reintroduced longboat, used strictly for pleasure, shouts of joy when a small boy lands a wriggling gudgeon and the slow whirring sounds of a couple of swans flying low over the fields by the river.

At night when the stars are bright, undisturbed by city lights, we lie flat on the lawn discovering a silent firmament above. Below is an equally silent valley. The activities of the past, the husbandry of the valley and building of its lovely villages have only enhanced this place known locally, and evocatively, as the Vale of the Nightingale.

Margaret Wilson, Murhill, January 1994

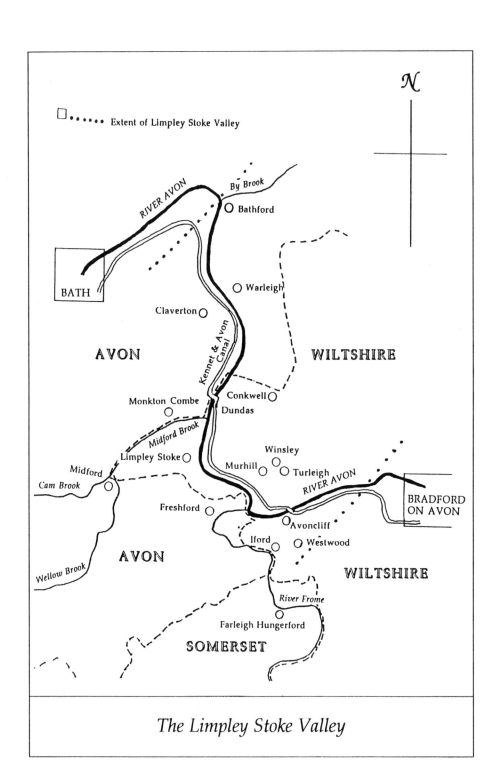

□ · · · · · · Extent of Limpley Stoke Valley

RIVER AVON

By Brook

○ Bathford

BATH

○ Warleigh

Claverton ○

AVON

Kennet & Avon Canal

WILTSHIRE

Monkton Combe ○

Conkwell ○

Dundas

Winsley

Limpley Stoke ○

Midford Brook

Murhill ○   ○ Turleigh

Midford

Cam Brook

RIVER AVON

BRADFORD ON AVON

Freshford ○

Avoncliff

Iford ○   ○ Westwood

AVON

WILTSHIRE

Wellow Brook

River Frome

Farleigh Hungerford ○

SOMERSET

The Limpley Stoke Valley

1 The Limpley Stoke Valley

The Limpley Stoke Valley straddles the boundaries of Wiltshire and Avon and also touches the neighbouring county of Somerset. It falls awkwardly across the corners of two Ordnance Survey maps and in recent times has been the subject of controversy as to its geographical location and extent. For a true definition of its borders I am guided by a resident who was born, lived and died in the Limpley Stoke Valley.

In 1961 Sir Hugo Marshall was Vice-Chairman of Bradford and Melksham Rural District Council and was also a Member of the Boundaries Commission. Sir Hugo, having an extensive knowledge of the valley, presented evidence for a review of local government areas. He spoke thus:

There has been a good deal of dispute as to what is meant by the Limpley Stoke Valley. I was born in the Valley and still live in it, at least I think I do, though it has recently been so variously defined that one cannot be sure of anything. I was particularly astonished at a statement made by Somerset County Council in their representations to the Commission. I quote 'In Somerset and Bath there is no uncertainty as to what comprises the Limpley Stoke Valley, it is the local name for that part of the Valley of the River Avon from the village of Limpley Stoke (from which it get its name) to where it flattens out between the villages of Bathford and Bathampton'.

I was surprised by this sudden certainty because about 3 years ago Bathavon R.D.C., in Somerset, when making their original representation to the Commission, asserted that the Valley began not at Limpley Stoke but at Freshford. I was astonished because I do not believe that any citizen of Bath standing anywhere in the village of Bathampton would consider himself to be in the Limpley Stoke Valley. Wherever the Valley may begin, there can be no doubt whatsoever where it ends. It ends on the one side of the Valley at Bathford, and on the other side of the Valley at the point where the sides of Bathampton Down suddenly turn through almost a right angle from running almost due east to running almost due south, namely the point on the Warminster Road A.36, known locally to everyone as the Dry Arch.

.....There has been a good deal of argument as to where the associations of the Valley lie, and for that reason I reiterate our contention that the River Avon flows through one continuous single valley from Bradford on Avon to Bathford. The hill that rises steeply above the right bank of the river at Bathford continues uninterruptedly and unbroken right the way round to Bradford, one unbroken wall of the Valley. On the left bank the wall of hills rises almost equally steeply, but this wall is broken in two places where the Avon's tributaries, the Frome and the Midford Brook, join it above Freshford and below Limpley Stoke respectively. Except for these narrow and winding valley entrances the only way out of the Valley on its left bank between Bradford and the Dry Arch, is to climb up its precipitous sides. A local man will think immediately of hills such as Brassknocker, Stoke Hill, the long grind on the A.36 to Upper Limpley Stoke, Staples Hill at Freshford or Becky Alley at Avoncliff.

It is our contention that one must look at this Valley as a whole and that looked at as a whole there can be no doubt where its associations lie, and that is with Wiltshire. Indeed to get from the Valley into Somerset one has got to climb out of it. If one sticks to the Valley one is led inevitably into Wiltshire. The railway line running along the Valley is a case in point. Where does it go to? It goes to Bradford where it divides, one branch going to Trowbridge, Westbury and Salisbury, the other to Chippenham or Devizes. The line from Bath into Somerset does not come this way at all, having tunnelled its way out of Bath it joins the Midford Valley and runs through Midford and Wellow to Radstock and Shepton Mallet.

As you can see Sir Hugo was a Wiltshire man and he felt the whole valley, as defined, would be administered more easily under one authority, i.e. Wiltshire. He was concerned that some of the villages would be absorbed into Somerset and indeed, at that time, Somerset had proposed that the whole Parish of Limpley Stoke and part of the adjoining Parish of Winsley should be transferred to Somerset.

Much water has passed along the Avon since then and a glance at an Ordnance Survey map will show that the county boundaries now run a tortuous route up hill and down dale, around villages, cutting through ancient parishes and crossing the river over the four miles between Bradford on Avon and Bathford, which I would agree is the Limpley Stoke Valley. Sir Hugo continued to live in Murhill, in the valley, in Wiltshire but looked straight across the valley to Freshford which is in Avon, but which used to be in North Somerset.

For the most part we can forget the county boundaries and concentrate on the landscape and its villages and hamlets. The limestone plateau with its horizontal strata through which the valley is carved is further intersected, as mentioned above, by the Frome and Midford valleys which flow into the Avon near Freshford and Monkton Combe, both of which will be explored. Other villages which climb its hillsides are Limpley Stoke – which gives the valley its name – Turleigh, Freshford, Winsley and Westwood, all of which are in or near the valley. The hamlets of Murhill, Conkwell, Warleigh and Avoncliff overlook the river. Alongside the Avon and running parallel with it for much of the way, are the Kennet and Avon Canal and the railway line. The valley is cut by one ancient road (the B3108) across its centre at Limpley Stoke, linking the A36 on the west side of the valley with the A363 to the east. Its crowning man-made glory is the two eighteenth century aqueducts which carry the water of the canal high over the railway and river. An eleven-arched viaduct takes road traffic across the Midford Valley.

The great historical importance of the valley and its surrounding area cannot be emphasised enough as it has played a central role in the life of this country from prehistoric times until the present day. Its fame is also related in no small part to its geological makeup and some of the names that were given to its geological strata are used world-wide. The man who first discovered the importance of relating fossils to the different strata, thereby having a profound effect on geological science, made his discoveries while living in the Midford Valley.

The River Avon, as well as being the vital force for the creation of the Valley has, for two thousand years, been a major trading route linking the Bristol Channel with the great Bronze and Iron Age civilizations inland and has continued to play its part through Roman times until now. The flat land of the limestone plateau through which the valley is carved is an integral part of the landscape. This is where the first inhabitants had their settlements and farms and where agricultural activities have continued through the centuries.

The geological phenomena in the Mendip Hills to the south, which created conditions for the half million gallons of hot water to gush out of the ground each day in Bath, also attracted prehistoric man. From the time of the Bronze Age, and possibly earlier, it is likely that a settlement grew up near the hot springs and from that time the fortunes of the valley people have been inextricably linked with those of Bath. It is impossible therefore to focus on the valley alone as in the last millennium and before – both Bath and Bradford have played a central role. The connection with Bath is very evident in Roman times. From 1000 A.D. and throughout the Middle Ages and beyond, Bradford on Avon, like Bath, emerges as a centre of religious, agricultural and industrial importance. Both will be explored in the following pages.

In 1953 the Federation of Women's Institutes set itself the task of encouraging its members to write a history of their own particular village. The result has been an invaluable historical record of village life through the centuries as recorded, and often remembered, by the inhabitants, past and present, of those villages. The gazetteer at the end of the book will include as many extracts from these histories as space allows. With the help of these and other chroniclers, geologists, archaeologists and historians it is possible to pull together the threads and make some sense of a small piece of England, the story of which began when shallow seas covered much of southern Britain.

Geology

One hundred and eighty million years ago, in the region that we know as Wessex, a cluster of crustaceans, crayfish-like animals, crossed the ripple marks of a sandy beach and headed for the warm sea. They joined a myriad of other sea creatures such as ammonites, trilobites and marine reptiles. In great swathes around them, attached to the sea bed by a 'root', strange animals related to sea urchins and starfish known as sea lilies, swayed to and fro filtering their food from the water by tentacles. These were the Bradford Encrinites (*Apiocrinites parleinsoni*). Time passed and it seems that the mass destruction of these sea creatures took place with an inrush of muddy clay which filled the area and the process of fossilization began.

In the late eighteenth and nineteenth centuries there was a great interest in the new science of geology and its relationship with evolution. The discovery of the section of fossilized sandy beach with its ripple marks and crustacean tracks and the fossil beds which contained these creatures was made near Bradford on Avon. The deposits where the fossils were found is known as Bradford Clay, a form of Oxford Clay dating from the mid-Jurassic period about 150 million years ago. It is interesting to note that the people who found time to study and observe the natural wonders around them such as geology, flora, fauna and archaeology were frequently clergymen or medical men. In this case three eminent surgeons in Bradford – William Fifield Ayde, James Pearce and his son, Joseph Channing Pearce – were the enthusiastic collectors of the local fossils. Joseph, who was born in 1775, started his interest in fossils when he was five-years-old. Perhaps he, like other children in Bradford, used the hard, spherical top of the encrinite as a spinning top (see exhibit in Bradford Museum). His large collection is now in the Bristol City Museum. Fossils from the Bradford Clay can be found in major museums all over the world.

The rocks which make up the scenery of the district we know today were laid down as sediments in the warm seas during the Jurassic period between 200 and 130 million years ago. The oldest rock is the Midford Sand (about 190 million years old) which occurs in the lower part of the Avon Valley around Limpley Stoke and the Midford Valley. The youngest rock known as Kellaways Clay (around 170 million years old) occurs at the surface near Broughton Gifford. Between these two clays lies the Great and Inferior Oolitic Limestone from which some of the purest building stone is quarried.

The flat limestone plateaux, which form the ridges of the valleys around Bath, were created from special geological conditions. Unlike the tilting limestone Cotswold hills further north, the strata here are horizontal and each plateau differs in height according to the height of the Great Oolitic limestone band. Beneath this top band of stone is an intervening band of Fuller's Earth clay. Springlines occur where the limestone meets the clay. The water undercuts the clay causing 'cambering' as the limestone above topples down hill. Below the Fuller's Earth

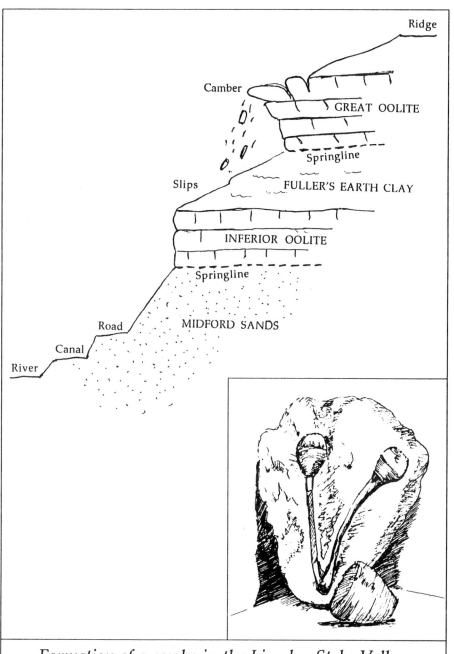

Ridge

Camber

GREAT OOLITE

Springline

Slips

FULLER'S EARTH CLAY

INFERIOR OOLITE

Springline

Road

MIDFORD SANDS

Canal

River

Formation of a combe in the Limpley Stoke Valley.
Inset: Bradford Encrinites
(drawn from an exhibit in Bradford on Avon Museum)

lies the Inferior Oolite which in turn lies on shale and sands, such as the Midford Sand. The Avon and its tributaries have cut through these weaker layers eventually creating a deep valley between the harder plateaux. The result is a magnificent series of deep river valleys or combes, the wooded slopes of which are made up of bands of limestone up to a hundred feet thick, enhanced by numerous springs emanating from the joints of the bands.

The limestone is made up of tiny round grains called ooliths, from the Greek words *oos* and *lithos* meaning egg and stone respectively. They were formed aeons ago in warm tropical seas when tiny shell particles were gradually coated with lime as they rolled around on the sea bed. Bath stone can be divided into two distinct groups and known in builders' terms as 'freestone' and 'ragstone'. In some local villages it is possible to tell at a glance how old a building is by whether it is constructed of ragstone (which includes fossils and is derived from surface quarries – stone which is not carved) or freestone (bearing no fossils and derived from deeper quarries, and which can be cut or carved in any direction). The change from one to the other took place about 1670-1700.

Two million years ago the Ice Age began. It was not one continuous era of Arctic conditions but was divided into four distinct periods with warmer times between. These interglacial periods allowed the spread of the type of trees we know today in our valley although they gave way to hardier trees such as pine and birch during colder times. At the end of the last phase of the Ice Age, the North Sea and the English Channel were still dry land and it was the gradual melting of the ice and the warming of the earth, a process which was to take four thousand years, that filled the seas and separated our island from the rest of Europe. During this time the land was filled with mighty forests and swampy river valleys inhabited by countless animals, birds and reptiles. In our own valley and surrounding area, glacial deposits from the Ice Age have revealed bones of the animals of that time (see exhibit in Bradford on Avon Museum). The Ice Age is thought to have contributed to the course of the Avon Valley, particularly the largely unexplained deviation into and through the Limpley Stoke Valley.

No description of the geology of the valley and its environs would be complete without reference to William Smith who came to be known as the Father of Geology, and whose story is told in a later chapter.

The Bristol Avon River

For the first time since its early tricklings we see the river flowing in a deep valley with hills rising steeply on either side. These hills are gladdened with woodlands, and woods and hills combine to make this 'Nightingale Valley' the loveliest stretch of the river. It is as lazy a pleasure as I know to lie in a boat, better I admit if it were a punt, but the only punting reach is over Saltford weir – somewhere below Limpley Stoke, drifting at a snail's pace with the slow stream. For preference let it be a summer's afternoon, when the haytime's here, and the mayfly is on the water; when the wild rose is in bloom and the air is fragrant with meadowsweet and rushes are flowering in the shallow pools, while the nose of the boat swishes through the tall, murmuring grasses. You are deep in a world of greenery. Shadows of cloud move across the opaque waters. Every now and then there is a clean 'plop' of a fish rising. The cookoo calls from the vault of heaven, now near, now far, and bids you rejoice with summer while you may.

This is a pretty fair description of what must surely be the most beautiful stretch of the River Avon in all its eighty-eight-mile length from source to sea. It is an extract from *The Bristol Avon* by Ernest Walls, published in 1927. The scene has changed little in the last sixty-five years and the same pleasure and peace that Ernest Walls found can still be experienced.

The Bristol Avon is so called to distinguish it from the various other Avons in Wiltshire, Warwickshire and Gloucester, the name actually meaning 'river' from the old Celtic word *afon*. Our particular river has its source in the Cotswolds and its mouth in the Severn Estuary. From its source on the Badminton Estate it follows a loop through the tilting (dip-slope) of the limestone for a distance three times that of the direct route to Bath. It flows north-east to Malmesbury, reaching the clay vale of North Wiltshire, where it takes a meandering course to Chippenham and drops south to Melksham. Just before Bradford on Avon it turns sharply west and north, forsaking the clay vale to meet again the limestone plateau where it carves its way through the Limpley Stoke gorge to Bathford. Here it is joined by the By Brook (which has its source close to that of the Avon but takes an easier route) before turning south west to Bath and on to Bristol.

The most unorthodox part of the Avon's course is between Staverton and Bath and its position continues to baffle geologists. Why, when a river is flowing south does it suddenly turn west and north, gouging its way through a wall of limestone to create a deep valley, before flowing west to join the Severn? At present, the theory is that during the Ice Age a great ice barrier had formed to the south and created a huge glacial lake known as the Trowbridge Lake. When this lake gradually melted, the overflow channel was directed northwards and, over thousands of years, carved out the Limpley Stoke gorge.

The river's catchment area is 857 square miles and many tributaries feed the Avon throughout its length. We are concerned only with the tributaries in the

Limpley Stoke Valley, namely the Frome (Somerset Frome) and the Midford Brook (fed by the Wellow and Cam brooks). The confluence of the By Brook with the Avon at Bathford provides a convenient marker for the western end of the valley. The Kennet and Avon Canal enters the catchment area near Devizes and runs twenty-two miles before joining the Avon at Bath. The impervious clays of the valley mean that after heavy rain there is a fast run-off resulting in rapidly rising water in the tributaries, and the river becomes swollen and forceful. This in turn cuts deep channels in the river bed resulting in further erosion and often giving the water a cloudy appearance.

River Avon flowing beneath the aqueduct at Avoncliff.

Between Bradford on Avon and Bathford three old milling weirs cut across the river serving to retain water. These occur at Avoncliff, Limpley Stoke and Warleigh where the water above the weir can be at least ten feet deep. Immediately below each weir the cascading water has gouged out deep pools where the water is slow to move on and is well aerated. These pools provide excellent habitat for fish. Fresh water mussels such as *unio timidus* and various river snails have been found in great quantities below the weir at Avoncliff and elsewhere and are an indicator of unpolluted water.

The lowland zone of the Avon shows much variation in water depth and in recent summers has dropped greatly in almost drought conditions. However within a few months, particularly during autumn and early winter, the valley, in the vicinity of Freshford and elsewhere, can be largely flooded. Fortunately the great variety of marsh flowers that thrive on the banks can tolerate both flooding and drying out, such as the creeping buttercup (*Rannunculus repens*) which thrives in great quantities. Here also are the typical riverside trees such as willow, alder and bushy grey sallow while the river provides a habitat for reeds, rushes, yellow water lilies and reed sweet grass. Amongst their roots and in the shade of the trees lurk chub, roach, gudgeon, bream, barbel, perch, tench, eel, pike and dace, most of which can also be found in the canal nearby.

Between Barton Farm and Limpley Stoke there are four sewage processing plants which are managed by Wessex Water. Each treatment works has its standard of purification set by the National Rivers Authority. Although water required for treatment purposes is not abstracted from the Avon, the effluent leaving the works is piped into the river which then carries on the purification process. Abstraction does takes place near Limpley Stoke where water is pumped through large bore pipes up the Midford Valley to the reservoir at Tucking Mill. Claverton Pumping Station is also capable of abstracting up to ten thousand gallons of river water per hour to keep the canal topped up.

Although this is one of the most beautiful stretches of the river it has many different calls on its use. As I write it is swollen with the autumn rains – a winding, gleaming, silver streak as it flows fast through the valley on a sunny November day. This is a day for long skiffs streaking down the fast-flowing current. Not often does the river near Freshford allow them a clear passage as it does further upstream near Bradford or downstream near Dundas. It is a day to walk along the river bank, stalking the ever present heron, watching the fallen leaves swirling in the current and ever hopeful of seeing the blue flash of a kingfisher.

Warleigh Weir.

2 Natural History

In the eighteenth and nineteenth centuries while Bath was enjoying its heyday as a social and artistic centre, a growing number of people who were attracted to the city were intent on widening their horizons of knowledge of the physical and biological world. These people had little if any scientific training but shared an innate curiosity and desire to explore and discover. Bath became a meeting place of minds, and these early 'thinkers' added greatly to the understanding and development of modern science.

Following the successful foundation of the Bath Agricultural Society in 1777 proposals were made for 'the Establishment of a Select Literary Society for the purpose of discussing Scientific and Phylosophical subjects and making experiments to illustrate them'. In 1779 the Bath Philosophical Society was formed. Members were able to discuss 'the Arts and Sciences, Natural History, the History of Nations or any branch of polite Literature'. Of the twenty-five founding members, eleven were to become Fellows of the Royal Society of London.

Interest in the flora and fauna of the British Isles was encouraged by people such as John Walcott (c.1755-1831), an Irish born natural historian and a member of the 1st Bath Philosophical Society. He wrote several books including *Synopsis of British Birds* (1789), *Indigenous Plants of Great Britain* (Bath 1778-9) and *Exotic Animals*. He followed the Rev.William Turner (c.1508-1569), clergyman, physician and botanist, known as 'The Father of English Botany' who, besides his famous 'herball', published books on Bath. Between the Rev. Turner and John Walcott came John Aubrey (1626-1697) and it is to him we owe the first considerable list of Wessex plants in his *Natural History of Wiltshire*. He confessed he was no botanist but wanted to see the listing of flora of every county, including his own. Until that time the study of plants was mainly the domain of the apothecaries when medical herbalism and the science of plants were one and the same.

In 1855 two clergymen, the Rev. Jenyns and the Rev. Broome undertook weekly explorations of the hills and valleys around Bath and subsequently founded The Bath Natural History and Antiquarian Field Club. Jenyns made a survey of Bath flora which was published in G.N. Wright's *Historic Guide to Bath* (1864). In it he noted that *Ornithogalum Pyrenaicum*, rare elsewhere, grew in abundance and was used as 'an asparagus substitute by poor people'. This beautiful plant

20

known as Spiked Star of Bethlehem does indeed have as its common name Bath Asparagus. It is found in woods in the valleys around Bath. A recent publication notes that: 'In 1975 it was still occasionally sold as asparagus in Bath, though the increasing sensitivity to conservation may discourage the outrage.' (Heather and Robin Tanner: *Woodland Plants*, 1981.)

The rocks and soil of any landscape dictate the types of plants and animals living in a particular area and eventually varieties develop that are peculiar to that environment. So it is with the hills and valleys around Bath, where the oolitic limestone has produced hillside pastures, deep-wooded valley slopes and flat ridge tops, all taking advantage of the lime-rich soil. There is a complete pattern to any green space, fashioned as it has been by centuries of woodland management, farming and landscaping. Limestone grassland is particularly rich in wildflowers although the long history of farming in the area has resulted in few of these grasslands surviving. There are pockets of ancient woodland which have never been clear-felled due to the steepness of the valley sides.

*Spiked Star of Bethlehem,
also known as Bath Asparagus.*

In order to protect the best wildlife sites, many areas of the valley are designated SSSIs – Sites of Special Scientific Interest –by the Nature Conservancy Council (now known as English Nature). There are at least twenty-six wildlife reserves in the county of Avon, two of which are in the Bath area, and these are managed by Avon Wildlife Trust. Brown's Folly is owned by the Trust and Tucking Mill Reserve is owned by Wessex Water and leased to the Trust. Together they highlight the wealth of natural beauty found around the valleys. At present Wiltshire Wildlife Trust has no wildlife reserve near the Limpley Stoke Valley. However, some of the fields around Winsley, Murhill and Limpley Stoke are particularly rich in wildflowers, especially orchids, and are detailed in a new book *The Wiltshire Flora* which updates the 1957 *Flora of Wiltshire* by the renowned botanist Donald Grose. The new book has resulted from an eight-year survey and mapping project by three hundred volunteers recording the plants found in the county and their distribution.

Brown's Folly Reserve

The Folly stands on the top of the hill above Bathford, high above the Avon. As the river turns towards Bath, the valley floor widens as the steep slopes fall away, before rising to the rounded top of Little Solsbury Hill to the north. Taking advantage of this magnificent site, a local landowner, Wade Brown, built the 'pepper pot' tower about 1845, although his reasons may have been a little suspect. It is said that he did not altogether trust the fidelity of his beautiful wife. She was particularly fond of hunting and in order to keep an eye on her during her rides in the valley he built the lookout. Despite fears as long ago as 1935 that the tower was unsafe, it has recently been pronounced to be structurally sound and, if money allows, may be opened to the public. The view from the top, particularly with the advantage of being able to look south and east, would be breathtaking.

The nature reserve was purchased by public subscription in 1972 and the area was increased in 1984. It now covers almost a hundred acres including Mountain Wood Plantation, Steep Wood, Prigley Wood, Quarry Wood and Ash Wood and a large section of Bathford Hill to the south. The quarries on the hillside have long since been worked out, the scars of the industry almost covered now by trees and scrub. Over the spoil heaps has grown delightful downland colonised by wild flowers and plants such as wild thyme, harebell and nine species of orchid – including the rare fly orchid.

A print of Bathford in 1845 shows the hilltop above the village to be almost bare of trees, although there is some ancient woodland on the lower slopes which still exists today. Secondary woodland of ash and sycamore now cloak the hillside and planted conifers are gradually being removed to be replaced with native trees. The old, dangerous and crumbling mines are home to the threatened greater horseshoe bat, a protected species. Ferns, fungi and spiders cling to the damp and exposed cliff faces, a scene found elsewhere in the valley, notably near the Murhill quarries and the exposed sheer rock face along the canal at Limpley Stoke.

Greater Horseshoe Bat.

Tucking Mill Reserve

This small but very special reserve is part of the circular Tucking Mill Trail, devised by the Avon Wildlife Trust, in the Midford Valley and is found close to the reservoir which now fills the valley of the Horsecombe Brook. It is no more than a beautiful meadow, rich in summer with a wonderful array of wild flowers which share the slopes with numerous anthills, a sure sign that for some time no machine has disturbed it. Cattle have kept the scrub and woodland at bay, grazing in autumn after the seed has set and the insects have finished breeding. The profusion of wild flowers growing on the lime-rich soil between May and September include ox-eye daisies, germander speedwell, yellow-flowered rock-rose and the stemless thistle. The bee and pyramidal orchids also thrive and later in the year field scabious and knapweed add purple hues to the lengthening grass.

Close to the reserve is Tucking Mill Wood, dominated by ash, field maple and beech. Dogwood and spurge laurel grow alongside spindle and in May bluebells, cowparsley, dog's mercury, yellow archangel and herb robert carpet the woodland floor. Other woods in the valley are Priory Wood, traditionally managed as a hazel coppice, and Beech Wood which is planted with fairly young beech trees and where Bath asparagus grows profusely.

Barton Farm Country Park

Nearer to Bradford on Avon is Barton Farm Country Park which extends one and a half miles between Bradford and Avoncliff. The thirty-six-acre park, which is designated as an Area of High Ecological Value, is a remnant of the farmland attached to the medieval buildings of Barton Farm. It is managed by Wiltshire County Council with help from Bradford on Avon Preservation Trust. The park provides a rich variety of habitats for wildlife as it encompasses the river, canal, woodland and meadows. Riverside plants such as meadowsweet, comfrey, and purple loosestrife line the water's edge. The meadows are cut for hay while some areas are left to encourage the growth of grasses and wildflowers such as cowslips, red campion and cow parsley.

A circular walk by the canal from Bradford to Avoncliff returns through Becky Addy Wood to the canal towpath. Some of the birds to be seen en route are swan, coot, moorhen, mallard, tufted duck, heron, grey wagtail and kingfisher. In summer, dragonflies and damselflies hover over water where swallow and willow warbler nest. Woodpeckers, finches, treecreepers, nuthatches and tits share the valley with twenty species of butterflies, including peacocks, speckled wood, blues, tortoiseshells, red admirals and brimstones.

The woods of the Limpley Stoke Valley are chiefly of mixed deciduous trees with oak predominating. There are stands of beech, notably in Murhill, and larch on the north-facing slopes above Freshford and near Dundas and Conkwell. The dark green of the yew, fir, pine and spruce, the shiny green leaves of the holly, abundant ivy, the fronds of last summer's hart's-tongue ferns and the yellowing catkins of the hazel provide colour in the winter woods. In autumn the fluffy seed heads of the clematis, known locally as old man's beard, gradually turn to pure white and in the sunshine of a cold winter's day resemble a fall of snow as the stems writhe through the hedges and strangle the trees beside the canal and in the woods.

There are hedges of hawthorn, blackthorn and maple, trees of alder, lime, hornbeam and willow along the river banks, ash and sycamore which are often found on the edge of coppices, conifer plantations on the south slopes around Conkwell and coppiced hazel woods at Claverton, Conkwell and elsewhere. All contribute to the rich variety of wood-

Old Man's Beard.

land found throughout the valley – woods that shelter wild garlic, wood anemones, primroses, honeysuckle, violets and bluebells and provide a habitat for insects, birds and other animals.

The special geological conditions which provide the habitat for certain varieties of plants also encourage mammals. In limestone country there are pockets of sandy soil which are ideal for burrowing and the sandy crevices below the outcropping limestone bands are home to badgers and foxes. The cliffs, quarries, caves and woods found throughout the valley provide suitable roosting sites for most species of British bats. The woods also shelter roe deer which were reintroduced into Wessex in the nineteenth century after near extinction in this area. Extinct since the last century is the polecat which used to inhabit the area. Grey squirrels are plentiful in the woods; rabbits and hedgehogs are few although beginning to increase in numbers. Smaller animals such as voles and stoats encourage owls, the nightly calls of which echo through the woods. It is many years since we have found a glow-worm, a delightful little insect, which we once popped into a jam jar as a night light in the nursery providing a magical childhood experience.

In January the trees vibrate with the first territorial tappings of the woodpecker, to be followed in March by the mournful 'yaffle' of its call as it flies from tree to tree. The brightly plumed pheasant now makes his appearance and becomes bolder as he flies in and tries to land with dignity before strutting around inspecting the garden. Many creatures are surprisingly tame. Last year a pheasant wandered into the kitchen, a couple of roe deer crossed the lawn looking for a succulent rose or vine, badgers often forage about in the dustbin and dig holes in the lawn and squirrels scurry along the top of the fence before leaping into the pine tree and showering us with pieces of cone. This spring a young fox stopped to gaze inquiringly at us while we were gardening before trotting away across the lawn.

Green woodpeckers, jays, numerous wood pigeons and magpies are among the larger birds that visit the garden and in winter try to share the bird table with the smaller birds. Tits of all kinds, including flocks of long-tailed tits, sparrows, wrens, robins, blackbirds and nuthatches are frequent visitors. Only occasionally do we see the song thrush, lesser spotted woodpecker and various finches. Flocks of redwing appear for a limited period in winter. In summer, buzzards soar high above the valley and kestrels hover with vibrating wings, eyes searching for any small moving object below.

For a few years it was a privilege to open the window at night and hear the song of the nightingale. In recent years it has disappeared and we long for its return. (It was heard in Midford woods in spring 1993.) It would arrive with great regularity in April and sing with its partner for about five weeks, its clear song heard above wind and rain in the Vale of the Nightingale.

Wild garlic.

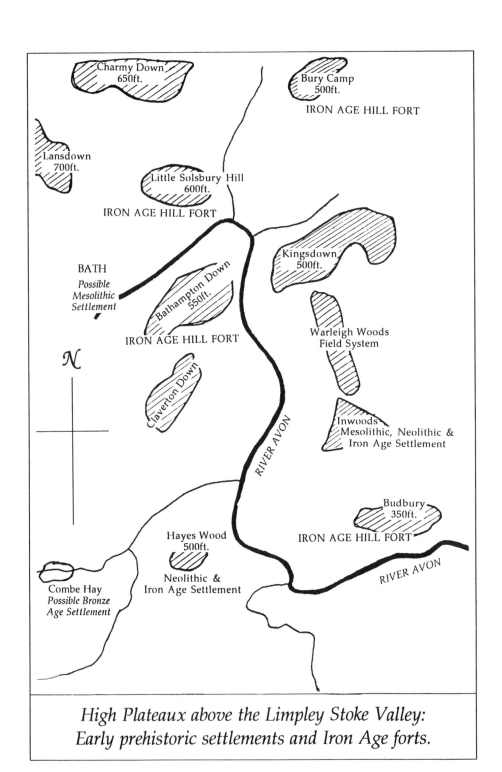

Charmy Down
650ft.

Bury Camp
500ft.

IRON AGE HILL FORT

Lansdown
700ft.

Little Solsbury Hill
600ft.

IRON AGE HILL FORT

BATH
*Possible
Mesolithic
Settlement*

Bathampton Down
550ft.

IRON AGE HILL FORT

Kingsdown
500ft.

Warleigh Woods
Field System

Claverton Down

RIVER AVON

Inwoods
Mesolithic, Neolithic &
Iron Age Settlement

Hayes Wood
500ft.

Neolithic &
Iron Age Settlement

Budbury
350ft.

IRON AGE HILL FORT

RIVER AVON

Combe Hay
*Possible Bronze
Age Settlement*

*High Plateaux above the Limpley Stoke Valley:
Early prehistoric settlements and Iron Age forts.*

3 Prehistory

Around the hills and valleys of Bath, including the area of the Limpley Stoke Valley, there are visible remains of man's occupation from the earliest time to the present day. Traces of Stone Age hunters mingle with the later Iron Age and Roman settlements. However, we have scant knowledge of prehistoric man and it was not until the millenium before Christ that man appeared in increasing numbers around the valley. The Saxon, Norman and Medieval occupation were the basis of the settlements we see today.

Although there is evidence that Palaeolithic (Old Stone Age) man inhabited the terraces of the Avon near Bath and Bristol and lived in the caves at Cheddar and elsewhere, the last phase of the Ice Age depleted the numbers of this early 'true' man. Then, for thousands of years, until the Norman invasion, there were migratory invasions of Britain from across the sea. The subsequent mingling of these different races from many regions of Europe resulted in the mixed blood and make up of the British people.

First they came over the land bridge from Europe following the retreat of the last Ice Age and the animals that were their prey – mammoth, reindeer and horse – and accompanied by countless common animals, birds and reptiles. The tundra gave way to pine and birch and, as the land became warmer, the trees and flowers that we know gradually emerged.

The implements these people brought had to be adapted to cope with the ever-thickening and extending forest, particularly after the separation of Britain from the continent around 5000 BC. The islands were now cut off from innovations taking place in Europe and Mesolithic man became even more isolated.

As G.M.Trevelyan writes in his *Shortened History of England*:

> For many centuries after Britain became an island the untamed forest was king. Its moist and mossy floor was hidden from heaven's eye by a close-drawn curtain woven of innumerable treetops, which shivered in the breezes of summer dawn and broke into wild music of millions upon millions of wakening birds: the concert was prolonged from bough to bough with scarcely a break for hundreds of miles over hill and plain and mountain, unheard by man save where, at rarest invervals, a troop of skin-clad hunters, stone-axe in hand, moved furtively over the ground beneath, ignorant that they lived upon an island, not dreaming that there could be other parts of the world besides this damp, green, woodland with its meres and marshes, wherein they hunted, a terror to its four-footed inhabitants and themselves afraid.

This was the landscape and these were the people who inhabited our valley and surrounding hills. Here in the alder-infested, tangled undergrowth of the marshy river valley we call the Avon, Mesolithic man survived as a hunter-gatherer. The garments he wore may have been made of pelts from beaver, known to exist in southern England at that time. The flint implements which he roughly fashioned and which were the key to his survival, would be developed over the next few thousand years into a precision instrument. In the south of England, particularly on the Marlborough Downs, flints lay on top of the soil but the bulk of them lay buried in the chalk. These early inhabitants became skilled stone miners, sinking deep shafts with picks and shovels made mainly from the antlers of the stag and scapulae of the ox.

Mesolithic or Middle Stone Age Man: 12,000 - 3000 BC

The very small flint implements which have been found in and around the Limpley Stoke Valley characterize the Mesolithic culture. At the beginning of this century, an interesting site near Conkwell was found to contain Mesolithic, Neolithic and Bronze Age flints and was indicative of a flint-working site of long duration. Most of the finds were taken to be housed in Bath where unfortunately they were destroyed in the Blitz. Others are in Devizes Museum.

At Haugh Farm near Winsley a Mesolithic stone scraper was found and in a ploughed field, also near Winsley, a greenstone axe was discovered. These and others like them have been small individual finds although more have been discovered nearer Bath. During recent excavations around the King's Bath spring in the city, implements thought to date from the Mesolithic period were found, giving rise to speculation of a settlement in the area dating from 5000 BC.

Early Neolithic or New Stone Age Man: 4000 - 2500 BC

The first farmers had arrived from the continent by 4000 B C and introduced a way of life that has persisted and developed to this day. Early Neolithic Man was still a hunter-gatherer and the change to the establishment of settled agricultural communities was gradual. He still used stone implements but he was on the verge of the civilizing influences of the use of metal. Hunters and farmers co-existed probably for a period of five hundred years. The Middle Neolithic period (c.2800-c.2400 B.C.) is regarded as being a time of change in the countryside with evidence of woodland clearance and new farming methods, notably the establishment of field systems found on the Carboniferous and Oolitic Limestone plateaux in the Bath/Bradford area. Settlements in the area would have been small-scale units or farmsteads. The area around Inwoods near Farleigh Wick shows evidence of these early farming methods.

Throughout the Neolithic period, flint and stone axes were used for forestry, woodworking and hunting. Pottery, which may have been made in the Bath/Frome area, was transported into Wiltshire. These movements of flint and pottery from east to west and west to east may have used a specific route along the Avon river as far as Bristol, a route that perhaps saw the transportation of the stone monoliths from South Wales for the building of Stonehenge in a later century.

Late Neolithic Period: 2400 - 2100 BC

Around this time it appears that the population dwindled although we have little understanding of why that happened. The forest regenerated in areas that had been cleared of trees, chambered tombs were blocked up or abandoned and only one settlement in the area – at Hayes Wood near Freshford – has yielded evidence of late Neolithic pottery. In 1935 J.F.S.Stone and A.T.Wicks undertook trial excavations at Hayes Wood and wrote up their finding in the *Somerset Archaeological and Natural History Society Proceedings Vol. 81*. They found flint flakes, animal bone and sherds 'which from appearance and texture recall Early Bronze Age or Neolithic Ware ... Later layers of the dig revealed 416 sherds from an Early Iron Age date ... dateable probably within the period 4th to 1st centuries B C.'

Beaker Period: 2100 - 1650 BC

At the close of the New Stone Age further immigrants from the Continent settled in southern England. They came from Holland and are known as the Beaker people. They buried their dead either in existing megalithic cairns or in newly constructed round barrows. Clay drinking cups or beakers from which they take their name were often inserted in the burial. Numerous beaker burials are found on Salisbury Plain and the Marlborough Downs around Avebury. In our area, the nearest of these burials was found on Charmy Down above Batheaston where, in a shallow oval pit, covered by a round barrow, a fine long-necked beaker and a small bronze dagger were found. It was the Beaker people who developed the henge (an earthwork with surrounding bank or ditch), added the standing stones at Avebury and transported the bluestones from Pembrokeshire for building Stonehenge.

The Bronze Age: 1700 - 650 BC

During the Bronze Age the area was intensively settled although surprisingly few artefacts from that time have come to light in the valley. The Bronze Age was a mainly settled period with great emphasis on the increase in farming, metalwork and trade. These people sought out the high, dry uplands and spread through Wessex from the Wiltshire Downs to distant Exmoor. The metal workers excelled in fashioning ornaments and implements, creating superb socketed spearheads, flanged axes and decorated dirks and rapiers. (See the Bronze Age Exhibit in Devizes Museum.)

There has been a concentration of finds on the hills around Bath culminating in an elaborate gold-covered bronze 'sun-disc' discovered on Lansdown, as well as a profusion of Bronze Age round barrows on the hills around Bath including many on Bathampton Down. In the valley a few individual finds have been made and further west, along the Cam at Combe Hay, we can speculate on the possibility of a Bronze Age settlement when the excavation of a Roman site revealed late Bronze Age pot sherds.

Undoubtedly the hot springs in Bath had attracted settlement to the area. The springs themselves were probably left untouched as a sacred place, hidden in the tangled undergrowth and difficult to approach, a place of steaming water gushing from the wooded hillside – a place of awe and wonder, best left to the gods!

Trade played an ever-increasing role in the lives of the people whether it was a bronze-smith peddling his wares across the countryside or the more sophisticated trade communication with Brittany and Central Europe. Connections with Ireland via the Bristol Channel are very evident from the plentiful supply of flat copper axes from south-west Ireland found around the Avon and beyond. There is no doubt that settlement around the Bristol Avon and Bath increased dramatically at this time.

These early people were known collectively as 'Iberians', a term used to distinguish them from the Celts – the tall, fair or red-haired folk who arrived on these shores during the Iron Age, only a few hundred years before the Romans. These earlier Iberian people were mainly dark-haired and despite their primitive and sometimes barbaric way of life they were not savages. Through the millennia of the Old Stone Age, the Neolithic and the Bronze Age, they raised themselves onto the first steps of civilization.

The Iron Age: 650 BC - 43 AD

It is to the site at Combe Hay that archaeologists turn in order to establish a date for the coming of the Iron Age in this area. Initially the discovery of pottery was thought to be of early Iron Age date but with the use of radiocarbon dating it is now thought to be earlier and that general Iron Age characteristics stem from this time. This pottery, which can be related to that found in Wiltshire, can be dated at between the sixth and fifth centuries BC.

It seems a paradox that the so-called Iron Age and its various stages and influxes of immigrants from Europe is generally sorted, put into groups and dated by its pottery rather than its iron tools and ornaments. Certainly the iron objects produced then add to our overall understanding of the lives of those people, but

Late Iron Age Pottery
100 BC - 50 AD

the shapes and decorations of the increasingly elaborate vessels and pots used by them provides the essential chronology of change.

The majority of people lived in small settlements, on farms and in small villages. Despite the domination of the Iron Age hill fort, many of which are found in Wessex, it is probable that more people lived outside its walls than inside. Three Iron Age hill forts stand sentinel at both ends of the Limpley Stoke Valley and it is interesting to speculate on whether these hill forts contained rival communities or whether together they formed a grand defensive plan against other tribes, strategically placed to provide defence from invasion from the river below. Certainly the valley was well defended with the presence of the forts on Bathampton Down and Budbury, both of which are roughly dated to between the eighth and sixth centuries B.C. The fort on Little Solsbury Hill is estimated to have been built between the sixth and second centuries B.C., its massive walls suggesting that its origins were defensive. In time this fort was settled and occupied by a farming community, with an emphasis on wool production which extended well into Roman times. To the north the Iron Age fort known as Bury Camp at Colerne is thought to be of a later date.

Some excavation of all the hill-top forts in the area has taken place but the detailed survey of Budbury Hill Fort, undertaken by archaeologists in 1969, has provided a picture of the life of the inhabitants of the valley in the last centuries before Christ.

Budbury Hill Fort

On a promontory high above the valley, the first known settlement at Bradford on Avon was constructed, an Early Iron Age hill fort corresponding in age to the fort on Bathampton Down, four miles to the north on the other side of the river (see above). An excavation of the Early Iron Age hill fort at Budbury in 1969 was intended to examine a burial mound before it was destroyed by development. Despite the discovery of the remains of a promontory fort of Early Iron Age date, probably enclosing about six areas, the building of houses continued inexorably to obliterate the last vestiges of the settlement. However, a careful examination of the hill revealed a double ditched promontory fort, rich in artefacts. The work was carried out by G.J.Wainwright and is described in detail in the *Wiltshire Archaeological Magazine, Vol.65.*

The bulk of the rampart, occupying a triangular spur projecting south into the Avon Valley, was 37 metres in length. It had already been destroyed by buildings and gardens before the dig took place. Of considerable interest was the discovery of a single house, 6.5 m. by 4.25 m. by 3.1 m. with an internal clay hearth and two internal partitions. In Britain the circular house was almost exclusively used throughout the Iron Age and the discovery of a rectilinear building at Budbury was a rarity. The house would have had a ridge-roof and been well plastered with daub.

Great quantities of Iron Age pottery were found together with domestic appliances and metal objects. Some 4,449 animal bones were identified, most of them split or chopped for cooking purposes. Spindle whorls and loom weights made from limestone, along with bits of bone comb, suggest the weaving of cloth.

Iron Age Man

Who were these early inhabitants of the Limpley Stoke Valley? In the last six centuries before Christ, Celtic tribes, originally from the area that we call West Germany and the Netherlands, overran much of Europe. Wave after wave of Celts invaded our island, entering from the east and south, subduing and pursuing the inhabitants, including some of their own peoples who had preceded them. They were tall and fair or red haired, skilful in the art of ironwork and other crafts. Agriculture, started in the Bronze Age, was further developed. Wheat was grown in the south and the presence at Budbury of saddle querns used for grinding corn suggests the preparation of cereals. They developed field systems and enclosures for cattle and they learnt the secret of fermenting grain with honey to produce mead consumed at ritual ceremonies.

Of the thousands of bone fragments discovered, the animals that are found to predominate are sheep, goats and cattle. These animals, besides producing food, suggest evidence of wealth among the tribes and were probably used as a means of barter. Other animals of importance to the tribes were the pig and the horse, the latter having symbolic significance and venerated as a deity, as well as being used for travelling at speed.

As well as human bones, domestic animals were found such as the dog and cat. Wild animals such as roe deer, red deer, hare, vole and various birds – duck, goose, dove, raven, rook and jay, as well as domestic fowl, were also found. The valley and the surrounding woods were inhabited by countless animals and birds. Great herds of swine wandered through the forests. Fish were abun-dant in the river below.

Although he dabbled in farming, Iron Age man had a varied life which included hunting and fishing, weaving, bee-keeping, metal work and carpentry. The fashioning of pots was becoming more intricate. 16,876 sherds of pottery were found at Budbury. (Pottery from Little Solsbury Hill included coarse jars and cordoned haematite-coated bowls.) Life was frequently disrupted by tribal wars and the making of flint-topped weapons and hunting tools was continually on the mind of the Iron Age warrior.

The emphasis placed on the warrior hero sometimes obscures the spiritual-ity of the Celtic people. The Celt felt his destiny had been pre-ordained and that death was the centre of life. Mysterious, ritual ceremonies took place with the merging of the fairy and spirit-world. There was an intermingling of the physical and supernatural world, particularly between the warrior and his Sun God and, above all, the recognition of water as the source of all life. All sacred wells, from local springs to great healing centres, such as *Aquae Sulis* (Bath), were under the protection of the threefold mother goddess who presided over birth, life and death. Such was the dedication to this fertility goddess that votive offerings – precious metals, skulls, weapons and domestic objects – were cast into rivers, wells and springs throughout Europe.

The river or stream was a living expression of the Earth Mother who was represented as a triad, a theme which frequently recurs in Celtic art and literature. It is interesting to note that a small Celtic sculpture of three mother goddesses was found on Bathampton Down, a short distance from the springs at Bath. The spring known for so long as Ladywell near Budbury may have been a Celtic sacred spring, one of the numerous streams that issue from the hillsides of the valley. The number seven also has a mystic religious significance, occuring fifty times in Revelations, and is particularly connected with water. The Turleigh Trows is a series of seven stone drinking troughs, possibly dating from Roman times or earlier. There is another similar line of seven troughs in Batheaston and at Gloucester Cathedral the washing place for the monks in the cloisters also has seven basins. (Information from G. Underwood: *Winsley Scrapbook*.)

Turleigh Trows.

Trackways along the ridges to link with other camps in the area would have been forged and, although it is impossible to prove their existence, it is interesting to speculate on where they would have run. Although the less densely vegetated ridge tracks would have made trading and transport easier, a way through the marshy valley bottom, perhaps making use of the river, cannot be ruled out. The Romans undoubtedly improved local existing trackways. Perhaps the Roman Fosse Way, which crossed the Avon and continued northward near Bathford, made use of an ancient Celtic trackway running past the Iron Age settlement at Bury Camp, near Colerne. Perhaps this Celtic route extended to the main trading route which stretched from the east across the Chalk Downs (the Ickneild Way) to the Severn estuary in the west and in turn linked the Iron Age settlements around the Limpley Stoke Valley with the great trading posts of Europe.

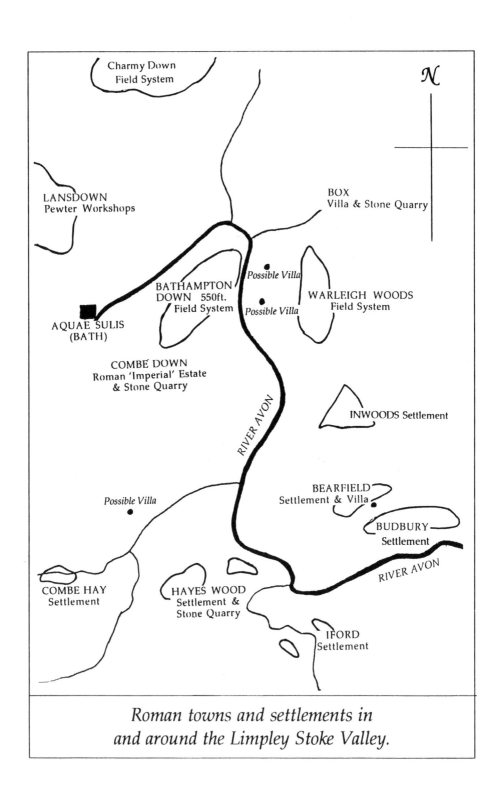

Charmy Down
Field System

𝒩

LANSDOWN
Pewter Workshops

BOX
Villa & Stone Quarry

Possible Villa

BATHAMPTON
DOWN 550ft.
Field System

WARLEIGH WOODS
Field System

Possible Villa

AQUAE SULIS
(BATH)

COMBE DOWN
Roman 'Imperial' Estate
& Stone Quarry

RIVER AVON

INWOODS Settlement

Possible Villa

BEARFIELD
Settlement & Villa

BUDBURY
Settlement

COMBE HAY
Settlement

HAYES WOOD
Settlement &
Stone Quarry

RIVER AVON

IFORD
Settlement

*Roman towns and settlements in
and around the Limpley Stoke Valley.*

4   History

The Romans

When the Emperor Claudius invaded Britain in AD 43 his task was not a difficult one, particularly in southern Britain. The first forays by the Romans to the shores of Britain had taken place a hundred years before and in the intervening century Roman traders from Gaul had settled in increasing numbers. Many of the tribal chiefs had become Romanized and national resistance was minimal. It was only as the Roman soldiers pushed west to the Welsh mountains and to the north that they encountered difficulties.

The efficiency of the Roman military machine and the method of conquest was quite unlike previous and indeed future invaders of Britain. Their expertise in the subjugation of a nation involved the systematic laying of military routes having strategic alignment and dotted with regular garrisoned forts for the troops along their length. In the early years the military outpost farthest west was the line of the Fosse Way which came from the south through Ilchester and crossed the Avon at Bath before running north through Cirencester. A likely site for a fort in the Avon valley is in the Bathwick area where various Roman artefacts have been found although a definitive location has not been established. The presence of a fort was thought likely after the discovery of a military cemetery on the north side of the city.

Nowhere in the south of the country is the system of Roman roads more evident than around Bath. There is a convergence of roads on the town which suggests that *Aquae Sulis* was more than a place of pilgrimage and a resort for the troops. In all directions roads led to other major towns, particularly to the port of Sea Mills near the Severn Estuary and Poole on the south coast and with links to other provincial towns. Although it was still used locally, the mighty Fosse Way, which was of such early strategic importance, became superfluous by AD 60 as the Romans pushed into Wales and the north. As London became a major port and grew in importance, the road to the north of Bath, running from Silchester to Sea Mills, linked London with the legionary fortress at Caerleon and the regional town at Caerwent in South Wales.

Other considerations, such as the lead mines on Mendip, led to the construction of a road from Charterhouse through the Chew Valley to the River Avon. Throughout the area many minor roads existed linking farms and villas to the wider road system. These smaller roads did not have the substantial engineering properties of the military roads and can only occasionally be identified, such as a small section near Freshford, now part of the Warminster Road.

Romano-British settlements and communities and the emerging 'villa' estates of the Romans in the area point to Bath as a thriving market town, fed with produce from the surrounding countryside. For centuries Bath was dependent on its immediate locality, particularly the Avon valley, to provide the necessities of life for an ever-increasing Roman population and its visitors. The hot springs, which the Romans were delighted to exploit, lay in fertile territory which was also rich in mineral deposits and good building stone. The stone to build the baths was mined locally from surface workings on Combe and Bathampton Downs, Box, and possibly a quarry at Hayes Wood. Its roof was lined with lead from the Mendip Hills. Coal from outcrops at Priston, Paulton and Newton St. Loe was burnt for ritual purposes on the altar of *Sulis Minerva* in the great Bath temple. For the Roman soldiers, some of them accustomed to the luxury of Roman society and homesick for fun and laughter under sunny skies, the discovery of the hot springs and the creation of the baths must have seemed a godsend. Here they were able to recreate the life they missed so much and Bath soon grew to be the centre of fashionable Romano-British society.

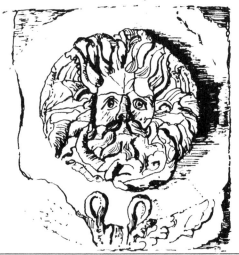

Sulis Minerva, Roman deity

The majority of people living in and around the valley were employed in the production and marketing of food. The field systems on Bathampton and Charmy Downs and near Warleigh Woods were probably used for growing cereals, the steep-sided valleys for grazing sheep, while the lush river meadows provided grass for cattle-rearing. Heavy taxation on grain production in the fourth century encouraged further grazing of sheep which is thought to have become the dominant feature of the countryside.

Although agriculture played a large part in the lives of most peasants they would also have been employed in the extraction of stone for building and the mining of coal to fuel furnaces for the smelting of iron on numerous settlements. The area was a centre for the manufacture of pewter using lead from the Mendips and tin from Cornwall. Excavations at Lansdown and also Camerton on the Fosse Way to the south of Bath, produced evidence of pewter workshops and perhaps the growth of a cottage industry would have provided local peasants with a small income.

A large 'Imperial Estate', retained under Imperial control for the supply of minerals and large quantities of food for the Roman army, has been suggested. It may have covered a wide area possibly involving Bathampton Down, Combe Grove and Horsecombe Vale escarpments and it is likely that the Estate had a controlling interest in the extraction of stone in the area.

From within the city walls the Romans attempted to 'civilize' the surrounding population. Although it had a social basis of slavery, in many ways it was a fairly liberal system of government. The tribal chief was given every opportunity to become Romanized, in language, dress and custom and in return be allowed to remain leader of his tribesmen. With Winchester so far to the east, Bath is thought to have been an administrative centre. The peasants were absorbed into the Roman villa estates which dotted the countryside. Once the more warring tribes such as the Durotriges in the south and the Dumnoni tribe in the far west had been subdued it was a time of relative peace, no doubt welcomed by the more compliant Dobunni tribe who inhabited North Somerset, Gloucestershire and parts of Wiltshire. The estate workers become no more than serfs tied to the soil but the population flourished under Roman administration.

Retiring Roman soldiers came to live in Bath or became farmers and landowners. In the first and second centuries they lived in relatively modest farmhouses (*villa rustica*) but by the fourth century the country villa (*villa urbana*) had come into its own and luxurious buildings of stone with intricate mosaic floors and elaborate heating systems appeared in great numbers – more than twenty-eight villas are known within a twenty-four kilometre radius of the city. One of the best preserved in the area, with splendid mosaic flooring, and almost palatial in size, is situated near the By Brook at Box. There is evidence of a villa at Bearfield north of Budbury with bath and outhouses. Two Roman settlements, close to the Avon near Bathford, have been discovered and there is more evidence of occupation at Combe Hay, Limpley Stoke, Iford and Hayes Wood. It is likely that many have yet to be unearthed. Budbury, Bradford on Avon, Winsley, Iford and many other sites have produced a variety of Roman artefacts, including stone coffins, skeletons, pottery and many coins.

During their excavations of the Neolithic settlement at Hayes Wood in 1935 Stone and Wicks also found evidence of Roman occupation and quarrying.

The ditches of the earthwork were hewn out of solid rock which made a convenient quarry for stone. The Rev. Skinner, who visited it between 1819 and 1826 considered it to be a Roman exploratory camp. He found Roman pottery within the enclosure but this may be explained by its proximity to a Roman site, 350 yards to the north in a field, Little Twinkeys, in the parish of Limpley Stoke which has yielded, since 1922, 23 coins of the 3rd and 4th centuries and large quantities of Roman pottery including Samian.

Another interesting find at Hayes Wood was the discovery of snail shells providing evidence of an item of food enjoyed in the first centuries AD:

The old turf line, 1 foot thick, contained a large number of snail shells. These were sent for identification and a special report was made on them. 12 species were represented. At least three of which are edible. There can be no doubt that they are food debris and judging from the differences in condition it is probable that many of them have been cooked... It has often been suggested that two of those species were eaten during Romano-British times but this is the first instance where it is certain that this is the case. All the shells are well developed and some examples are very large. It has been suggested that more congenial conditions prevailed in the Romano-British period.

During his Iron Age excavations at Budbury, Wainwright found evidence of a Romano-British settlement. Coarse-ware pottery and a few Samian fragments were found, representing pottery from that time:

The flanked bowls, late cooking pot and other sherds acceptably fall into the period late 3rd/4th centuries A.D. and with further certain evidence lacking this period is suggested for the Roman occupation of the hillside.

Romano-British pottery vessels
1st - 4th centuries AD.

Religion played an important part and in Bath the temple was dedicated to *Sulis Minerva*, a bringing together of Celtic and Classical deities. From all over the Empire pilgrims flocked to the holy town. But it must be remembered that beliefs and traditions die hard and the discovery of a carved relief of a threefold Celtic mother goddess on Combe Down, a short distance from the sacred springs, suggest that Celtic customs flourished through the Roman occupation. Although there is little evidence of Christian worship it seems that Christians and pagans tolerated each other, some having joint beliefs.

By the second and third centuries the valley was alive with settlements, farmsteads and villas. Trees had been cleared and trackways forged or improved providing easier journeys to the market at Bath. The hills around the valley, particularly Bathampton Down, had been extensively cultivated and many more sheep, cattle and pigs grazed the slopes and valley floor. The Bristol Channel and the River Avon provided an essential link with Ireland, Wales and the Continent for the import and export of goods. Flat-bottomed boats transported cargoes, including the fine building stone, downstream from Bath to the important Roman port of Sea Mills and returned with imports such as wine, olive oil and fruit for local consumption.

It was a time of industry and prosperity. *Pax Romana* prevailed.

Sub-Roman Britain: *c.* 400 - 600 AD

By the fourth century Roman Britain had reached its highest level of sophistication but the provinces now faced a threat from Barbarian raids, particularly from Ireland. The Barbarian Conspiracy of A.D. 367 saw the partial or complete destruction of villas particularly near the Bristol Channel and penetrating up the Avon as far as Keynsham. Many villa owners, scared by these raids, now preferred to move from their isolated estates into the relative safety of Bath. It is possible that at this time the walls around the city were strengthened and that it had its own defence force. Some of the hillforts in the area appear to have been re-occupied.

At the same time the heart of the Empire in Rome was weakening due to attacks nearer home. Fewer and fewer Roman legions could be spared to serve in Britain and the great exodus of the Romans began. In 410 A.D. came the official end of the Roman occupation when Rome refused to answer a call for help, telling Britain she was now on her own.

In the following centuries the success of the Roman occupation proved to be transient. For one thing Britain was too far from the Mediterranean to be permanently influenced by a Mediterranean civilization. The only people trained to fight were the Roman legions who made up the regular army and once they had departed Britain was easy prey for any invader. The Nordic tribes who were to conquer Britain, had a more lasting impact by displacing the Celtic tribes and introducing German, Anglo-Saxon and Scandinavian peoples who had allied languages and religion, and common art forms. They brought with them the religions of *Thor* and *Woden*, words taken up and used by both English and Germans for days of the week.

The settling of these races in our islands were barbaric times and for two hundred years, from the end of the fourth century, very little is known. During this time the invader, with his warrior's wooden shield, his boar-shaped helmet and his spear-head, conquered Britain and reduced it to the Dark Ages.

Of the fate of Bath and the consequences for the surrounding area we know a little more. Much is revealed from the silt and mud which choked the Roman Baths in the Third and Fourth centuries. The excavations of 1965-8 and 1981-3 examined the two metres of soil which incorporated the history of seven hundred years, from Roman to early medieval times. It seemed that the mud that eventually destroyed the baths was caused by a rise in the water table. The ensuing floods from the Avon backed up into the culverts which drained the baths. Lack of financial resources to solve the problem of the growing threat from abroad eventually brought about the collapse of the baths as the flood-waters took their toll. The area, lying low in the town, was reduced to little more than a marsh with ruins projecting from it. However, the town itself continued to be inhabited through the dark centuries until the coronation of King Edgar in 973 AD when Bath once again emerges into the light.

Floods in the valley.

It was some time during the eighth century that an Anglo Saxon poet gazed with wonder on the fallen stones in the marsh that had been the baths and was inspired to write a poem which he called 'The Ruin':

> *Wondrous is this masonry, shattered*
> *by the Fates. The*
> *fortifications have given way, the buildings*
> *raised by giants are*
> *crumbling. The roofs have collapsed, the*
> *towers are in ruins...*
> *There is rime on the mortar. The walls are*
> *rent and broken away,*
> *and have fallen undermined by age.....*

The rising of the water table meant that the River Avon, rushing through the Limpley Stoke Valley, would have been wider, fuller and marshier than today. The falling birthrate and a devastating plague depleted the community in the town as well as the countryside. However, there is nothing to suggest massive depopulation but with a collapsed economy and government, frequent raids and an uncertain future life would have been distinctly unpleasant.

Anglo-Saxon Britain

In about 442 the Saxons who had settled in Southern England renewed their barbaric practices by sweeping through southern and eastern England, plundering and pillaging as they went. It is not known whether they reached Bath; somehow the west managed to remain independent, quelling the raids and defending the towns.

Although lack of dating evidence makes it approximate, it was at this time that the great defensive earthwork of Wansdyke was thrown up by the Britons to stop the Anglo-Saxon advance from the north.

A definitive review of Wansdyke was undertaken by the historian Lady Aileen Fox in 1958 in an article entitled 'Wansdyke Reconsidered.' Previously the great Iron Age Camp on Bathampton Down was thought to have its outer wall incorporated into the dyke but Lady Fox is adamant that the dyke ends a little above the source of the Horsecombe Brook.

> There is no doubt that the earth-work ended, as on the west of the plateau, a little above the springhead (of the Horsecombe Brook) and the 500 ft. contour, but the actual terminal has not survived the modern building developments.... There is no evidence the Dyke went further.   (*Archaeological Journal* Vol 115, 1958)

During the sixth century the Saxons advanced further west and in 577 won a decisive battle at Dyrham north of Bath, thus gaining the three important towns of Cirencester, Gloucester and Bath. Some fifty years later, perhaps as a reprisal for land taken from them after the Battle of Dyrham, the Britons fought and lost to the Saxons at Bradford on Avon in 627 A.D. It is recorded in the *Anglo-Saxon Chronicle* that Cenwalh, King of Wessex, fought at *Bradenforde be afue* (the broad ford on the river). This was probably a battle for control of the river, important as it was as a boundary and trading route.

Bradford on Avon in Saxon Times

The Saxons who founded Bradford soon had control of the River Avon. The settlement which had started on the south bank spread to the north where it is thought a monastery or abbey was founded, possibly in the vicinity of the little Saxon church. The existing Saxon church in Bradford on Avon is almost certainly a replacement for the one built as part of a complex of monastic buildings by

St Aldhelm around 700 AD. It is said by William of Malmesbury to be dedicated to St Laurence. The original Saxon church may have been in wood and the existing stone building put up in the tenth century but experts cannot agree. Whatever its age it is a gem of a church and the Saxon builders have earned our gratitude for its existence.

Stone carving, Saxon Church, Bradford on Avon.

Bath in Saxon Times

At the time that St Aldhelm was building his monastery in Bradford, a nunnery was being founded in Bath. According to a twelfth century copy of the foundation charter of Bath, Osric, King of the Hwicce (a sub-kingdom of Mercia), established a convent in Bath in 675. In 757-8, it is further recorded, a grant was made to the brothers of the monastic church of St Peter. By 781 the monastery was described as 'most famous' but the nunnery was not mentioned again. From that time the monastery received numerous benefactions and being a building 'known to be of wondrous workmanship' was, on May 11th, 973, the scene of the coronation of Edgar, first King of all England.

Somerset was certainly at the heart of national events and trends in late Saxon times and important early Christian centres were almost certainly present in the seventh and eighth centuries at Glastonbury, Wells and Bath, the latter holding estates which included Bathford, Monkton and Woodwick (a deserted village near Freshford). Unfortunately, little archaeological evidence is available, particularly at Glastonbury, as a catastrophic fire in 1184 destroyed the earlier monastic buildings. At Wells very little has been done in the way of excavation although there is good evidence for a late Saxon Cathedral. Bath awaits the collapse of its Abbey before proper excavations can take place. I remember attending a lecture given by Professor Barry Cunliffe in the late 1970s and saw the gleam in his eye as he contemplated the possibility of tearing down the Abbey in order to excavate the Roman temple of *Sul Minerva* and the later monastic buildings!

The Danes

Before Alfred the Great's final victory over the Danes at Ethandune in 878, Danish armies and raiding parties overran the west country. There is a strong local belief that a battle took place in Winsley. However, any available evidence, such as weapons supposed to have been found during the building of the modern village, has long gone. What is now known as Dane Bottom was always, until this century, Dean Bottom.

There is also a tradition that a Danish raiding party led by Canute came up the Frome River to Bradford and set upon the destruction of the monastery in 1015. This was speculation on the part of William of Malmesbury who, in *c.*1125, gave an account of the foundation of the monastery and mentions St Aldhelm's little Saxon church. However in Malmesbury's day nothing was left of the monastery and he was uncertain as to whether it had been destroyed by the Danes or by the English 'in a greedy carousal' (VHCW).

In 955 the royal property of Bradford was bequeathed by the king to St. Mary's Monastery, Winchester. Four years later a great council was held at Bradford at which Dunstan was ordained a bishop. When King Edgar died in 975 Dunstan, now Archbishop of Canterbury, and politician as much as priest, took on the role of king maker. Edgar's son Edward was crowned in preference to his half brother Ethelred. Edward was subsequently murdered and Ethelred came to the throne.

These historical details are interesting because in 1001 Bradford was granted by King Ethelred to the abbey of Shaftesbury to salve his conscience for the murder of his brother.

> In honour of his brother St. Edward the Martyr, and in order that the nuns of Shaftesbury and the relics of the martyr should find at Bradford an impenetrable refuge from the attacks of the barbarians [*i.e.* the Danes] (VHCW).

The gift included not only Bradford but also South Wraxall, Atworth, Holt, Winsley, Westwood and Wingfield. As will be seen this event had far-reaching effects on the town and neighbourhood for the next five hundred years.

1000 AD - 1300 AD.

As the waters of the Avon continued their inexorable flow through the valley, the towns of Bath and Bradford, situated on its banks, followed similar paths of development as they emerged from Anglo-Saxon to Norman rule. Both had monastic buildings of importance in the Anglo-Saxon period and both lived in fear of further Danish raids which it seems eventually overwhelmed the monastery at Bradford and possibly also that at Bath.

Neither town seems to have been greatly disturbed by the Norman invasion and the framework of parishes, estates, villages and administrative boundaries laid down by the Saxons developed as the population increased. The Domesday Survey records Bradford as one of the principal boroughs in Wiltshire. The Hundred of Bradford, an administrative district with boundaries that fluctuated considerably over the next thousand years, had its origins before the Norman Conquest. Its inhabitants attended the Court of the Hundred of Bradford. (The Hundred is still in existence to some extent in the judicial and licensing district of Bradford magistrates and where the phrase 'Bradford and District' is used). Religion continued to play a vital role providing important ecclesiastical and administrative divisions and the church dominated the lives of most people one way or another.

An entry in the Domesday Book of 1087 records that the religious community owned seventeen of the villages surrounding Bath as well as a third of the town. Bath flourished in the eleventh century under the great prelate-statesman, John de Villula, Bishop of Tours, and the Episcopal see was moved to Bath when John of Tours became the first Bishop of Bath and Wells. For the religious community Bishop John built a huge Norman church on the site of the famous but now derelict Saxon church. He also set about restoring the baths and turning the town once again into a medicinal centre.

The Monastery in Bradford, as we have seen, was destroyed probably by 1015. In the Domesday Book, completed just twenty years after the Battle of Hastings in 1066, in part to document the extent of the land to be portioned out to the newly arrived Normans, we see that it states 'The same church [Shaftesbury] holds Bradford'. As in Bath, the Normans built a new church close by the little Saxon church.

The excavation of Budbury hill fort by Wainwright provided evidence of occupation after the Iron Age. There was evidence of Roman occupation and the presence of

> medieval and post-medieval pottery demonstrates limited occupation of the area in the 12th and 13th centuries and the presence of at least one occupied house or farm in the 14/15th centuries. The abundance of 17th/18th century sherds may also imply at least one occupied house at that date.

The Early Middle Ages

The turning point in the fortunes of the two towns and their surrounding villages was the introduction of weaving which started in England around 1333 and was soon to be established in Bath. Although the parish of Bradford and the valleys of the Avon and the Frome are more often connected with the wool trade, the citizens of Bath took to the trade enthusiastically at the expense of ecclesiastical demands. However, with the the Bishop's seat being transferred back to Wells, the Abbey buildings and baths fell into disrepair and during the next two or three hundred years Bath went into something of a decline.

Meanwhile the little town of Bradford with its unusually large parochial acreage (then about five thousand acres) was to grow and prosper under the jurisdiction of the Abbey of Shaftesbury until it was, in the fourteenth century, the largest town in Wiltshire apart from Salisbury, Malmesbury and Marlborough.

The Later Middle Ages

The chief centres in the region for the important undyed broadcloth production were in West Wiltshire and Somerset, particularly at Bradford, Frome and Bath and throughout this period the wool trade was the dominant industry in the valleys. Fortunes were made, great houses built, and churches extended and glorified. The demand for stone was enormous, bringing further employment and prosperity. Traditional industries, such as cheese-making, malting, brewing, fishing and wild-fowling were pursued by many families who were able to combine these activities with cloth-making. The population expanded and trade increased.

Religion and religious institutions continued to dominate English life and the immense changes wrought by the dissolution of the monasteries and the Reformation were to be sudden and shocking. In all, fifteen monastic houses in Wiltshire were dissolved, among them Hinton Charterhouse when the Prior and sixteen monks surrendered the priory to Henry VIII in 1539. Wealthy merchants and local gentry purchased the monastic sites and land, dividing up the estates, tearing down the buildings and selling the materials to pay for their purchases or using the stone for new buildings. Stone and tiles from Bath Abbey were used to repair churches and houses in Bath. Only the ruins were left as a legacy to the great monastic estates which had survived seven hundred years. The remains of Hinton Priory stand in a field just south of the Warminster Road.

The division and sale of these estates brought a new and wealthy land-owning gentry. Their elegant houses, surrounded by parkland, are still a feature of the Wessex landscape. A new era of English country life had begun. Local government was reformed; justices of the peace were chosen from the landed gentry which meant that it was now these families who effectively controlled and administered each county. It was at this time that the 'county' became an important focus of local pride. Lord Lieutenants were appointed to be responsible for the defence of the county, providing arms and supervising the muster of armed men. Although this was primarily for defence of the country against a foreign invader, its importance became evident in the Civil War which was to follow.

Stiff leaf foliage on reeded corbel, Hinton Priory.

The Civil War

Wessex became a battleground in the Civil War, the struggle between Charles I and Parliament in the seventeenth century. Major skirmishes took place in the region. At the time of the civil unrest Farleigh Hungerford Castle was in the hands of the monachy, Sir Walter Hungerford having been executed for 'treason and unnatural vice' in 1540. Sir Edward Hungerford, the rightful heir,

> commanded the local forces of Wiltshire for Parliament (with little credit) in 1642–45, while his half-brother John was a Royalist, and was put in charge of a garrison at Farleigh late in 1644. The garrison was dependent on Bristol, and on 15 September 1645, four days after Prince Robert had surrendered Bristol, Sir Edward reduced Farleigh, apparently without bloodshed. He seems to have occupied the castle both before and after it was held by his brother.
>
> *(Farleigh Hungerford Castle*: Department of the Environment)

Several personalities in and around Bath emerged as natural leaders, inspiring resistance of North Somerset to the Royalist invasion. One was the Rector of Claverton, known as a firebrand puritan, who deeply regretted that the lord of the manor, Sir William Bassett, had become a Royalist. Another was the clothier, John Ashe, who had made a fortune from the wool trade and gave huge sums of money in support of Parliament. He conducted a brilliant propaganda campaign at the start of the war.

On July 2nd, 1643, Sir Ralph Hopton had led his army of Royalists from Wells to Bradford on Avon. He approached Bath on the north side of the Avon expecting to do battle with the Parliamentarians led by Sir William Waller. Godfrey Laurence in his book *Bathford Past and Present* describes the events that followed:

> Meanwhile Sir William Waller had ranged his army on Claverton Down commanding that bank of the Avon. In order to command also the opposite side he bridged the river below Claverton Manor and sent Colonel Burghill with a large force of cavalry and foot soldiers under cover of darkness to the top of the wooded slopes of Warleigh where Bathford adjoins Monkton Farleigh.
>
> Thus early on the morning of 3rd July 1643 the royalist cavalry advance-guard fought their way through the ambush and with the rest of their army pursued Burgill's force along the ridge and down through Bathford. Simultaneously the royalists, seeing Waller's artillery challenging them from Claverton Down, sent their Cornish foot soldiers through Warleigh, down to the river. After a skirmish, in which a number of solders were killed, they took the bridge as darkness fell. Waller, seeing that the royalists now commanded the river crossing, withdrew in the dark to Bath.
>
> At midnight the Earl of Carnarvon, Sir Ralph Hopton, and other royalist commanders considered taking up an advantageous position on Lansdown but instead decided to quarter for the night at Batheaston to allow time for the Cornish foot to rejoin after the fighting for the bridge at Warleigh.

Claverton Down, a strategic position in the Civil War.

This was to be a grave mistake for, when they reached Lansdown the following day, the Royalist army found that Sir William Waller had beaten them to it. The whole Parliamentarian army had dug itself in on the ridge during the night. All through the day of July 5th, 1643 the two sides fought a long and bloody battle. Despite grave losses, and the serious wounding of the leader of the Cornish infantry Sir Bevil Grenville, the Royalists managed to seize Waller's earthworks. Waller's army took up a new position and the two armies bombarded each other through the evening. During the night Waller withdrew his army to Bath for rest and refreshment and at dawn, with heavy losses and low morale, the Royalists called off their attack. Sir William Waller, the Parliamentary General, claimed an outright victory.

A week later Sir Ralph Hopton, in command of the Cornish force, went on to do battle at Roundway Down near Devizes and there overthrew the Parliamentary forces. But eventually the Royalists weakened and in 1649 Charles I was imprisoned and beheaded. For fifteen years there was a break in the power of the monarchy during which time loyalty to the Crown manifested itself in various ways, one of which was the ill-fated uprising in Wiltshire in 1655 led by Colonel John Penruddock. In 1660 the restoration of the monarchy was welcomed in the region but many people had been impoverished by the War, particularly from the lawless bands of soldiers whose unruly and destructive behaviour wrought havoc in the countryside.

Georgian England

During the seventeenth century Bradford was in the forefront of industrial change and growth. In the textile trade there was a readiness to grasp the introduction of innovative weaving methods and produce a new type of cloth called 'medleys'. Instead of the heavy hard-wearing broadcloth, the market was now ready for lighter cloth of different colours. The 'medleys', pioneered and developed in Bradford, and other new ideas, such as worsted cloth from Ireland, which was finished and marketed in the West County, ensured the continued prosperity of the textile trade in the valleys.

This was the period of the great names in the industry – Methuen, Yerbury, Ashe, Shrapnell and many others – which continued down the centuries. During the seventeenth and eighteenth centuries their great houses enhanced the area and their social standing tied in neatly with Bath society which at that time was becoming, for the second time in its history, the most fashionable social centre in England.

Although agriculture was still the biggest employer, the textile industry was a close second with most people being involved in some way. However, the developing technology saw the introduction of machines such as the spinning-jenny and the carding machine bringing with them a real fear of unemployment.

The Industrial Revolution, and the never-ending supply of stone from the quarries, fuelled the construction industry which played a huge part in the growth of the area. Canals, railways, roads and houses brought people and employment and profoundly affected the lives of most people. Other innovative ideas took root. William Smith, the 'father of geology', produced his stratigraphical map of the area. Fossil collecting and geological theories were more than a passing interest to many and the first Geological Society was set up under the guise of the Bath Philosophical Society. Ten of its founding members were to become Fellows of the Royal Society.

The building of Bath and the long reign of Beau Nash, who taught the rules of good behaviour to fashionable society, had far reaching effects on the civilizing of the nation:

> It was the special function of the Eighteenth Century to diffuse common sense and reasonableness in life and thought, to civilize manners and to humanize conduct. (G.M.Trevelyan: *A Shortened History of England*)

The growth of fashionable society in Bath in the eighteenth and nineteenth centuries provided the setting for the meeting of minds, and the town became a hotbed of scientific discoveries: the musician turned astronomer, William Herschel, whose telescopes and work *Construction of the Heavens* contributed so much to the development of modern astronomy; Sir John Harrington from Kelston was responsible for an important technological invention – the water closet; The Rev. Thomas Malthus who lived in Bath and is (probably) buried at Claverton, did pioneering work in his *Essay on Population* published in 1798. The Rev. L. Jenyns, a clergyman and naturalist, founded The Bath Natural History and Antiquarian Field Club in 1855. He made a survey of Bath flora and claimed that 'the only plant peculiar to Bath and not indigenous to any other part of England is *Euphorbia Pilosa*, which he found in a wood on Claverton Down and in a lane near Bath' (*Flora of Wiltshire*). He and the Rev. C. Broome made regular weekly forays into the Limpley Stoke Valley and around Bath.

Many visitors who came to Bath for treatment stayed and added to the list of inventors and discoverers, such as Dr. George Cheyne FRS, who became a Bath physician. His *Observations on Gout and on Bath Waters* went through seven editions in six years. Dr. William Falconer FRS, who was a physician at Bath General Hospital between 1784-1819, wrote *An Essay on the Bath Waters* and was revered as a scholar and physician. His other interests were theology, botany and natural history. Edmund Rack (1735-1787) settled in Bath in 1775. He published articles on agriculture and theology and founded the Bath Agricultural Society in 1777. Today it is famous as the Royal Bath and West of England Show.

Towards the end of the eighteenth century the exceptional circumstances which brought so much employment to the area must have, for a while, cushioned the effect of growing poverty and hardship which was to become rife in the nineteenth century. As the cloth industry declined in the face of growing competition from the north, the huge rise in population in Bradford and Bath contributed to unemployment and distress. Changes in farming practice, severe winters and poor harvests towards the end of the century brought matters to a head, leading to increased taxation and poor relief.

Victorian England

By 1750 most towns and large villages in Wessex had a workhouse or poorhouse for the destitute. These were now extended or rebuilt. In 1834 an Act was passed grouping parishes into 'unions'. The Bradford Union included the parishes of Freshford and Westwood, the largest workhouse, or Union House, being at Avoncliff. By the 1840s many people had moved away in a desperate search for work, some emigrated to America and many others ended up on poor relief or in the dreaded Union House. Records show that an additional four hundred paupers, skilled workers in the cloth trade, were admitted to Avoncliff in 1841. Hunger was commonplace and suicides rose sharply.

The economic life of the towns and villages in the Avon valley took an upturn with the coming of the railways. As the network of routes increased farmers could distribute their produce to remote areas, afford to buy new equipment and make use of innovative farming methods such as artificial fertilisers and improved breeds of sheep and cattle. The biggest market throughout the region was for milk, supplying the increasing population of London. As market gardening became popular, national markets were found for fruit, flowers and vegetables.

The Court, Avoncliff (now called Ancliff Square):
home of the former Bradford Union Workhouse.

There was also a massive growth in the holiday trade. Spas, which had been popular since the seventeenth century, saw a great revival in the nineteenth century. Health Resorts were opening up and at Limpley Stoke the West of England Hydropathic Establishment was founded in 1860. On the hill above Dundas Wharf, with a magnificent view, was the Claverton Hotel, which no longer exists. By local tradition this hotel was one of 'ill repute' and had a reputation of entertaining passengers of the earliest 'pleasure' craft.

With growth in the economy the population expanded once again. The Church of England was overwhelmed by church interest and activities. The Victorians undertook a huge programme of repair and expansion of the existing parish churches. A large proportion of churches in Wessex have Victorian additions or were completely rebuilt as in the case of Bathford, Claverton and Monkton Combe. Winsley church was rebuilt except for its fifteenth century tower and Freshford has a Victorian chancel and vestry.

Many small communities saw a rapid growth in non-conformist churches. Chapels of various denominations have their place in most of the villages. John Wesley had visited Bradford early in his career as an evangelist and he first preached to an audience of a thousand at Bearfield in 1739. Thereafter John and his brother Charles preached frequently in the area, setting up the Bradford Circuit in 1780 which included more than thirty places in Dorset, West Somerset and North Wiltshire, one being the chapel attached to Turleigh House. In 1767, during one of their many visits to Freshford, John preached from a table set up near the churchyard. He describes in his Journal how:

I had no sooner begun to speak than the bells began to ring by the procurement of a neighbouring gentleman. However, it was labour lost as my voice prevailed and the people heard me distinctly.

Bradford remained head of its circuit until 1884 and the society is now associated with that at Trowbridge and Bradford Circuit. The churches frequently provided some general education as well as Sunday School and collectively they had a great social effect on the community, setting up friendly societies, temperance movements and funding charities, all with missionary zeal.

The Twentieth Century

Not so long ago, certainly well within this century, most of the villages around the valley had become social and economic islands and could meet the demands of everyday existence. Bakeries, tailors, dressmakers and cobblers were commonplace. Stone masons, wood sawyers, builders, local road sweepers, grass cutters and even lamp lighters had their place in the village. Now, even the petrol station, which was such a convenience, has gone along with the hardware store which cannot compete with the DIY superstore. As we blunder towards the end of the twentieth century, with recession and unemployment everywhere, will villages, through force of circumstances, again become more self-support-ing?

To many, this sense of unity is appealing. Villages, particularly in this area, are well supplied with community projects and there is also a growing interest in cultural activities. An increasingly high standard of music, drama and art is being produced locally. Westwood is one of many villages with a thriving art group; plays and music at Winsley, Iford, Westwood and Freshford have been immensely popular and a local school has been chosen as the site for the West Wiltshire Music Centre. Recently, sell-out performances of the Bradford on Avon Community Play and a spectacular production of the choral work 'Carmina Burana' in the Tithe Barn, have involved numerous people from local villages. Concerns and problems are already arising from the growing attractiveness of village life and for this reason a village plan, delineating the boundaries of each village and having respect for the green belt, is essential.

Tangible evidence in the valley of the two world wars is found in the inevitable village war memorial crosses and tablets and stained glass windows in the churches in memory of the dead. From the 1939-45 war, numerous defensive pill boxes still stand incongruously in the river valleys. There is one to the west of Avoncliff below the railway, another covered with brambles and almost invisible on the north side of the aqueduct. Others can be found near Freshford on the Frome and in the Midford Valley.

The First World War produced an abrupt break with the past and its secure timeless country ways that were never to return. Farming had been labour-intensive and for the farmer his world was one of horses and carts, unpaved roads and dusty tracks, old stone cottages and oil lamps. The physical makeup of the valley appears unchanged and unchanging, yet the break with the past is complete. Outside those steep, wooded hillsides, away from the river and its quiet meadows, beyond the vale of the nightingale and the peace and beauty of a unique English valley, the world rushes by.

Second World War pill box and 125 Intercity train near Avoncliff.

.... In the Middle Ages the lives of the people of Wessex and no less the inhabitants of our particular area were dominated by four influences – the church, wool, stone and agriculture. Tangible evidence of the interaction and reliance of one upon the other has come down through the centuries, providing the valley with its beautiful rural landscape, its villages, its churches, its houses of great variety and its agricultural buildings. Without the woollen trade Wessex would not have prospered in this way. It was the wealth created from wool that provided the money for building, and it was the quarrying of the local stone that provided the material for this building throughout Wessex and beyond ....

5 Valley Churches and their Origins

An autumn morning: mist rising from the river quickly covers the fields and gradually fills the whole valley. From the north side looking south only the highest trees can be seen meeting a hazy blue sky which promises another sparkling autumnal day. The wooded slopes are an echo of reality behind the diffuse cloud. Out of the fog can be heard the sound of church bells and as the waves of mist thin and lift, Freshford church appears and seems to float like a building from the celestial city. One might almost be forgiven for thinking this was indeed heaven.

The bells of this church have sounded their invitation to worship since the early 1400s, ringing their way across and up and down the valley joining with those of the other villages. In the Middle Ages one was rarely out of sight of a church tower or spire and never out of earshot of the bells.

The importance of religion to rural communities, as elsewhere, in the Middle Ages cannot be emphasized enough. The church dominated a parish not only by looking after its spiritual needs but also as a powerful economic influence. As a major landowner and founder of markets and fairs it had a hand in everything, employing vast numbers of people and benefiting enormously from the wealth created by the population. From Norman times to the Reformation it changed the landscape of England with its churches, monastic buildings and magnificent cathedrals.

Social life in the parishes was dominated by the church and gave rise to various ancillary buildings such as the Church House or meeting place. Here social gatherings, such as feasts, revels and money-raising activities, took place. These were very similar to our own present day charity-raising activities which still take place in Church Rooms up and down the country. But in the Middle Ages discussion would not have centred on the Sudan Well Appeal or the RNLI but on how best to raise money to glorify, extend or even rebuild their church in the modern style – a much more daunting prospect for the average villager. An example of a Church House dating from the sixteenth century is Old Church House (Trinity Church Hall) in Bradford on Avon built by Thomas Horton with profits from the wool trade. Indeed, in the land of the sheep, many great benefactors who had made their money from wool provided the funds for the building of the local churches.

The siting of an early church is open to speculation. The medieval village church is often considered to be the true ancient heart of the settlement and in many cases this is so. Sometimes the church developed from Roman beginnings, possibly originally from a site of pagan worship or an early 'celtic' settlement where there was a feature such as a holy well or cross. The little church of St. Mary's, Limpley Stoke is thought to have been started as a chapel in 1001. The church guide states that 'this is one of the Pear Tree Churches built to mark the position of a boundary pear tree, which had been planted by the Abbess of Shaftesbury to mark the limit of her land.' But there is also evidence that this site was a Roman settlement and possibly had already been a site of worship. Indeed near the west and south walls of the church 'is a very old curved stone boundary wall, which is supposed to mark the site of an ancient Holy Place'.

The forces of good and evil were ever present from early times. The protection of the church against the Devil was a genuine and abiding need so the building, decoration, structure and siting of the church were all important if virtue was to overcome vice. We are reminded of this by a tale attributed to the Anglo-Saxon builders of the early eleventh century. The legend of the 'Devil of Limpley Stoke' found in the Shaston Chartulary, dated 1322, is typical of the belief in the powers of darkness. It states that the Saxon builders 'commenced to build a church in a field down in the valley called Crockford, on the east side of the river, but that every night, the Devil, or some other ghostly form, came and removed the stones to the top of the hill. After persevering for some days, the builders resolved to use the site thus appointed.'

St. Mary's is now found high on the hill as far away as possible from the Devil-haunted river valley. In the early sixteenth century a winged demon was carved above the font in the parish church at Westwood and is known as the 'Old Lad of Westwood' or 'the Devil of Limpley Stoke'. An inscription underneath reads 'Resist me and I will flee'.

St. Mary the Virgin, Westwood

The origins of Westwood church are quite likely to have been of pre-conquest date. The earliest part of the church is the chancel. Its simple construction of small stone slabs and lack of elaborate medieval stone carving and small lancet windows in its south and north walls suggest it was built in the twelfth or thirteenth centuries. The ancient priest's door on the south side has a trefoil-shaped arch let into a single large slab of stone. The strange irregular carvings on the slab are probably Anglo-Saxon and the slab could have been one used from an earlier site.

Both the exterior and interior of this church are very beautiful. It has an incomparable setting, originally being one of three buildings with the medieval Manor house and the priest's house (which was demolished a hundred years ago).

'Westwood Lad' and font
in Westwood Church.

The only entrance is through the door in the tower, itself the chief glory of the church. It is one of a group of splendid Wiltshire and Somerset church towers built from the profits of the wool trade in the fifteenth or early sixteenth century. It is richly decorated with parapets, pinnacles, tracery and gargoyles (one of which fell in 1960 narrowly missing the vicar) and was probably built by a group of masons who specialized in these glorious edifices and who may also have built the chapel in the church. A distinctive feature of the tower not found in others in the group is the spiral staircase on the south east corner which is topped with an intricately carved stone cupola. This cupola is repeated in wood as a font cover in the nave of the church.

The nave, which was rebuilt in the late eighteenth century, has a remarkable moulded ceiling which fits surprisingly well into a medieval church. The pulpit, dated 1607, had been found by Canon Jones, famous for his discovery of the Saxon church at Bradford in 1840. It was found whitewashed and abandoned at Tellisford and may have come from Norton St. Philip.

Visit this church during its flower festival week, stand half way up the nave and be overwhelmed by its beauty, particularly the carved wooden ceiling of the chapel and the rare medieval stained glass in the east window. The oak carving on the pulpit, lectern and the rail behind it, as well as the more modern pews, are highlighted by the beautifully executed flower arrangements.

St. Mary the Virgin, Limpley Stoke

For me St. Mary's at Limpley Stoke is the most captivating of the valley churches. We know it is of Saxon origin because of the weather-beaten arch which stood for a thousand years in the main wall of the building and was clearly the entrance to the Saxon church. The Normans added a porch and probably the chancel to this small chapel and decided to retain the older arch. It is now part of a modern south aisle within the church.

Last year on Christmas Day a throng of us gathered in this church on the hill for early morning worship. The sun had just risen and its rays penetrated the traceried window throwing coloured light first on the Christmas roses and holly that filled the stone font before highlighting the horseshoe archway of the Saxon doorway, set incongruously and delightfully in the modern south arcade. Opposite the arch three stone steps lead to a recess in the north wall which for centuries has been used as pulpit. As we left the church we passed under the arch and through a simple 13th century Norman doorway to the churchyard where crumbling tombs from the thirteenth and fourteenth centuries flank the path to the church gate. A thousand years of worship and a Christmas morning to remember.

It is interesting to speculate on the age of these two churches dedicated to St. Mary, standing a mile apart, one of definite and one of probable pre-Conquest date. Together with the Saxon church at Bradford on Avon they are certainly the oldest in the area and stand as a tribute to the stone masons of those and later times.

St. Mary the Virgin, Limpley Stoke.

St. Swithun's Church, Bathford

Was there a church at Bathford before the Norman Conquest? In 1791 Collinson, in his *Antiquities of Somerset*, described the building existing at that time.

> The church is an old building, eighty feet in length and 20 in breadth, consisting of a nave, chancel and porch, all tiled [meaning stone tiled roofs]. At the west end is a square tower, containing two bells. The nave of the church is divided from the chancel by a clumsy Saxon arch.

What appears to be a Saxon stone coffin is now incorporated into the outside wall of the Lady Chapel. Built into the east wall of the churchyard are some Norman arch stones and a piscina.

In 1140 Archbishop Theobald refers to 'the church at Forde'. Bathford was then part of the estate of Bath Priory and some time 'between 1173 and 1181 Reginald Fitz-Jocelin, Bishop of Bath, set apart the revenues of the church at Forde for the maintenance of the priory at Bath'. (G.Lawrence: *Bathford Past and Present*)

An engraving of the church by T. Bonner was published in 1784. In his book on Bathford, Godfrey Lawrence speculates on whether or not this engraving bore any resemblance to the original church and whether or not it was altered or rebuilt. Subsequent alterations took place in 1753, 1818, and a new tower was completed in 1842. In 1870, except for the north aisle, the church was completely rebuilt and a new tower added in 1880. To this almost entirely Victorian church an extension to the north aisle was added in 1911.

It now stands proudly, crowning the village and looking down on houses much more ancient than itself, presenting a fine picture if viewed from across the valley. From the churchyard there are splendid scenes from this northern end of the valley looking towards Little Solsbury and the hills beyond.

The Parish of Freshford

In 1232 Ela Countess of Salisbury founded Hinton Priory for Carthusian monks. This was to be a major ecclesiastical influence in the area and the Priory gradually acquired land in the nearby parishes of Woodwick and Freshford. At the time of the Domesday Survey in 1086 Woodwick, a community which once existed between Hinton and Freshford, was part of the estate of Bath Priory. Perhaps the Prior of Bath built the church at Woodwick. Certainly there was one in existence in the thirteenth century. The first reference to Freshford church was in 1318 and both churches would have consisted of nave and chancel and be of appropriate size for two small settlements. By 1377 Hinton Priory had acquired the manor and patronage of the living of Woodwick and also a mill on the Frome which belonged to both communities. By the fifteenth century the two churches had amalgamated and gradually Woodwick, its church and commuity disappeared.

St. Peter's, Freshford

In his booklet on Freshford church Alan Dodge suggests the site of Woodwick church was in the field called Church Powels, just off the A36 and about three quarters of a mile west of St. Peter's church. He wonders if at this time Freshford church was rebuilt, as certainly the existing tower dates from then and is similar to the tower of St. Thomas à Beckett at Widcombe built in 1490.

In the early seventeenth century growth in the cloth industry brought wealth and a rising population to Freshford and the north aisle of the church was constructed. Again at the beginning of the eighteenth century considerable rebuilding and extension took place and many memorials in the church commemorate well known clothiers of the time.

During the rebuilding and extension of the Perpendicular chancel in 1859, a gallery was removed and a vestry built. At a time when hymn singing for all was introduced into churches in England a small organ was fitted. The increased literacy resulting from the opening of the church school encouraged participation by the congregation.

St. Peter's, Freshford.

Alan Dodge writes that

the whole status of the ecclesiastical parish of Freshford changed in 1970 .... when St. Mary's, Limpley Stoke was joined to the living. Then in 1976 .... St. John the Baptist at Hinton Charterhouse was also incorporated in the one ecclesiastical parish.

Although not strictly within the confines of the area under review a mention must be made of St. John's at Hinton Charterhouse. It existed before the Priory was founded in 1232 and has a Norman south doorway. The tower is either Norman or early thirteenth century but the top of it was renewed in 1770. The chancel, south chapel and the porch are all thirteenth century and there are good examples of lancet windows of the Early English period. At the end of the nineteenth century the present windows were inserted into the north aisle and contain some interesting local historical figures within the stained glass.

Across the fields to the north of the church are the ruins of Hinton Priory. Standing alone amidst the parkland is the Chapterhouse with its sacristry next to it, the undercroft of the refectory and part of a guest house. The Priory itself was destroyed at the dissolution although excavations have revealed a square cloister (226 by 226 feet) around which were fourteen small houses with walled-in gardens for the Carthusian brothers. Even at a distance the thirteenth century characteristics are recognisable in the three lancet windows on the east side of the Chapterhouse. Inside it is rib-vaulted in three bays, the vaults resting on reeded corbels which display stiff-leaf foliage. Ancient steps rise to the library above and the sun, shining through the deeply splayed lancet windows, produces a strange and lovely light on the stone of the vaulting of this old room of learning.

St. Mary's Church, Claverton

Claverton church first appeared in records in 1250 but this is not the church we see today. It was rebuilt in the fifteenth century and the present church, built in 1859, is a replica of that building with the addition of the north transept, erected later. From the older church has come the Scratch or Mass Dial (a sundial showing the hours of Divine Service) now fixed, upside down, to the wall of the porch. The fifteenth century church was covered inside with coloured frescoes, some of which came to light during demolition in the nineteenth century only to be immediately destroyed in spite of the Rector's protests. A water-colour copy of the fresco, painted by the Rector's daughter, now hangs in the church.

The mausoleum that honours Bath's famous entrepreneur from the eighteenth century brought fame to the tiny country church. Ralph Allen frequently visited his friend Richard Graves at Claverton and his desire was that he should be buried, not at Prior Park, his famous Bath mansion, but in a small churchyard overlooking the Limpley Stoke Valley. While digging the foundations of Ralph Allen's tomb in the churchyard, four skeletons of soldiers killed in the battle of Claverton in 1643 were discovered and identified by their uniforms.

Ralph Allen's tomb, St. Mary's Church, Claverton.

The church was reopened on January 1st, 1859, a charming solitary building approached up a steep path between high ancient stone walls. Various sections of graveyard surround the church, and the mausoleum and graves are separated from the magnificent parkland below Claverton Manor by a low stone wall.

St. Nicholas, Winsley

Winsley seems to have arrived a little later on the ecclesiastical scene. The first mention of a church in the community is a reference to a chapel which was cited in 1349 'when the vicarage of Bradford was ordained in that year. The chapel was granted, with the parent church, to the Dean and Chapter of Bristol in 1542 and in 1553 was said to have three bells.' In 1628 a curate lived in the house which had been annexed to the chapel 'and he enjoyed all small tithes except those of lambs. These tithes, which were of coppice wood, pigs, wool, 'cow white', calves, apples and the issues of two mills, were of a value not exceeding £10 a year' (VHCW).

The original church of St. Nicholas dates from the fifteenth century. Except for the tower, the church was demolished and a new one built in 1841. The tower, which has a plain parapet and is topped by an interesting saddleback roof, is connected to the new building by a covered passage. Until about twenty years ago a bell tower sat on top of the saddleback roof, topped by the weather vane. The fifteenth century font was restored to the church after being discovered in a garden in 1876.

In 1846 Winsley became part of a new perpetual curacy and a new parish, that of Winsley and Limpley Stoke, was formed in 1868 under the patronage of the Dean and Chapter of Bristol in the Diocese of Salisbury. Limpley Stoke is now part of the parish of Freshford and Winsley's sister church is St. James of South Wraxall. This church also has a tower with a saddleback roof which is repeated on the square stair-turret.

Right: St. Nicholas, Winsley.

St. Michael's, Monkton Combe

A short way up the Midford Brook is the church at Monkton Combe.

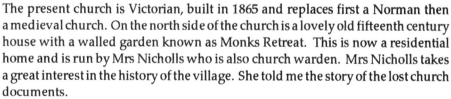

The present church is Victorian, built in 1865 and replaces first a Norman then a medieval church. On the north side of the church is a lovely old fifteenth century house with a walled garden known as Monks Retreat. This is now a residential home and is run by Mrs Nicholls who is also church warden. Mrs Nicholls takes a great interest in the history of the village. She told me the story of the lost church documents.

The Rev. Percy Warrington was one of those characters without whom life would have been the poorer for those who knew him. He was a philanthropist whose philosophy of life was 'rob the rich and give to the poor but make sure there is something over for the giver'! For some years he lived in great style in a mansion called Waterhouse on the south side of the valley in the parish of Freshford before being required by the Bishop to live within his own parish. Church documents of importance, instead of being kept in the church, were taken home to Waterhouse.

Later in his life, when he formed the Percy Warrington Trust, Waterhouse become a residential home and Percy himself died there in 1961. There was a clear-out of his possessions and, for better or worse, they were all heaped onto a bonfire. A painter and decorator, Mr. Tracey, who was working at Waterhouse at the time, passed by. Seeing a leather-bound book that had fallen clear of the flames, he picked it up and took it home. He was unable to read the 'Old English' and put it in a cupboard. Twenty years went by. Freshford Historical Society became interested in the history of Monkton Combe and its church. Mrs. Nicholls, a member of that Society, had been searching for the church documents for some time. Word reached Mr. Tracey and he produced the 'old book' he had put away years before. It turned out to be the old Baptisms and Burials Register, dated 1561. In the book are several interesting briefs or collections, one in particular for the 'repairing and beautifying of Paul's church in London' in 1661. Obviously this referred to St. Pauls after the great fire of London. The cover of the book had previously been restored by Richard Shute in 1826 who also began on its translation. Further restoration and translation have been undertaken by Freshford Historical Society and the book has been photographed and put on microfilm.

That was not all. 'A man from Gwent' now enters the story. This man worked closely with an older tradesman and it is probable that both men were working as joiners at Waterhouse at the same time as Mr. Tracey. The older man died and left the tools of his trade contained in a large box to his younger colleague. The younger man discovered at the bottom of the box three or four old books, some of which contained Monkton Combe Vestry Minutes and one in particular, which was the Monkton Combe Churchwarden's Accounts Book dated 1756. This young man realised the books were of some importance and brought them over from Gwent to deliver them personally to Mrs. Nicholls. Presumably these books were intended to be consumed by the flames of the same bonfire and these too were rescued by another tradesman. (The story of Percy Warrington continues in a later chapter.)

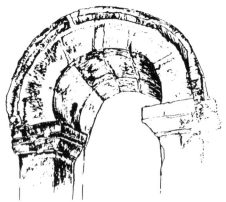

Saxon arch, St. Mary the Virgin, Westwood.

6 Valley Industries

Agriculture

Agriculture, the principal land use in the West Wiltshire countryside, is currently undergoing a significant period of change as a result of Common Agricultural Policy (CAP) reforms, uncertainties over world market prices, surplus production and changing consumer demands. The manifestations of this change are the steady decline in the agricultural workforce, set-aside land and limited 'on the farm' employment opportunities.   (*West Wiltshire District Plan*, February 1993.)

For the first time in its long history, farming in West Wiltshire, although still an important economic activity, now has a decreasing role to play. From pre-historic times to this century it has shaped and fashioned the Wessex landscape and nowhere in England is more evidence found of the dramatic extent of early farming practices, especially on the chalklands to the east. Early agriculture in and around the Limpley Stoke Valley has been explored in a previous chapter and shows that prehistoric man grew crops, raised stock and laid out field systems. These early fields were square or rectangular, about half an acre in size and were presumably used for arable cultivation.

The Romans farmed large estates, kept sheep and grew varied crops in and around the valley and it seems likely this would have continued well into Anglo-Saxon times. After the Norman invasion of 1066 much of Wessex was dominated by great estates belonging either to the Crown, the bishoprics of Salisbury, Winchester and Wells or to the great monastic houses of which the Abbey of Shaftesbury was one. Shaftesbury continued to hold the manor of Bradford which included South Wraxall, Atworth, Holt, Winsley, Westwood and Wingfield.

In 1281 the king claimed the manor of Bradford against the Abbess of Shaftesbury, saying that Richard I had been seised of it. Judgement was given in favour of the Abbess and in 1293 she was granted free warren in the demesne lands of Bradford. (VHCW)

An estate held in 'demesne' meant that the land was possessed and held by the owner and in the case of Bradford the owner was the Abbess of Shaftesbury, until the Reformation in the sixteenth century. The records kept at that time provide evidence of the workings of those great estates and is supplemented by the Domesday Survey of 1087. An inventory made of the parish of Bradford includes the following:

> In 1086 there was land for 40 ploughs in Bradford. In demesne were 8 ploughs, with 9 serfs and 18 coliberti. There were 36 villeins, and 40 bordars (a villein of the lowest rank) with 32 ploughs. There were 22 swineherds. On 'servient' (land acquired and worked in servitude) rendered 7 sextairs of honey. There was an arpent (a measure of land – about an acre) of vineyard and 50 acres of meadow. The pasture was 11 by 3 furlongs, the wood half a mile by 2 furlongs. The whole manor with its appurtenances was worth £60. (VHCW)

The Domesday Survey does little to describe farming methods although it gives some indication of the type of animals kept. Sheep were of major importance in the region and goats, kept for their milk and the production of cheese, were numerous. Dairy farming, which later was to become famous in the well-watered clay vales, was recorded in the Frome valley and was presumably becoming established in the Avon valley.

Haycutting at Freshford.

The twelfth and thirteenth centuries were the boom years of demesne farming, a time which saw numerous improvements in techniques and an increase in productivity. The population expanded, with a consequent extension of settlements and demand for food, leading to higher prices. There was great pressure on the land, woodland was cleared and arable farming extended as more and more land was brought under the plough. It was a time of prosperity and growth in Wessex.

In Medieval times the open field system came into effect, forming a common field system. The open field would be divided into blocks of land known as furlongs and each farmer would hold single strips within the furlong. In the southern Cotswold and northern Mendip parishes, territory was laid out in strips to include equal portions of hilltop and vale as well as the slope between the two. This system may have applied in the Limpley Stoke Valley. On the hills around Bath and particularly on the slopes above Warleigh, strip lynchets, the adaptation of strip fields to steep slopes, survive. The dating of these lynchets is uncertain but it gives the impression that the landowners and farmers were using every available method to produce grain and other crops.

Before the Enclosure Acts of the later Medieval period almost everyone living in the countryside had some land on which to grow crops and raise livestock. One tenth of all produce was donated as tithes, and in the case of the parish of Bradford these tithings boosted the coffers of the Abbey of Shaftesbury, which had become the richest nunnery in England:

> In 1349, seventeen years after permission had been given for the appropriation of the church by Shaftesbury Abbey, the vicarage was ordained. Thus were allotted to the vicar all oblations and small tithes from the town of Bradford: the tithes of wool and lambs and of all grain grown in gardens, curtilages and orchards there; the tithes of all mills; herbage and pasturage arising from all churches and chapels pertaining to the parish of Bradford, the tithes of lambs and wool and all oblations and small tithes from chapels of Winsley and Holt, all tithes, small and great, and all other profits from the chapel of Westwood. (VHCW)

The lush grass of the valley floor would have been used for spring grazing and later in the year for haymaking. The wooded hillsides accommodated the need for pannage, the exercise of common rights for grazing, such as the farming of pigs, which was widespread. Geese farming was also a possibility on the marshy land. This is known to have taken place in the Avon Valley at Broughton Gifford (Pamela Slocombe: *Wiltshire Farm Buildings 1500-1900*). Growing teasles for use in the cloth industry would presumably have been of great importance. Teasles grow sporadically in the valley today but they are not the same species as those used in the wool industry.

From Norman times until the eighteenth century, pigeons provided both eggs and meat, particularly in winter when lack of food for livestock meant destroying the animals. By the mid-seventeenth century numbers of dovecotes in England may have reached 26,000. Most estates kept large numbers of birds, particularly on monastic farms such as Barton Farm where pigeon holes are found in the farm building. Besides food, their dung was a useful manure and also a source of saltpetre for gunpowder. Their number declined partly because of the vast amount of grain they ate and eventually, by law, only the lord of the manor could house them.

Part of the demesne land would have been used exclusively for the lord of the manor for hunting deer (Claverton), keeping rabbits in warrens (Bathampton Down), and fish in ponds, particularly on the springline adjacent to the limestone outcrop (possibly at Limpley Stoke). Warrens were frequently referred to in medieval documents as the rabbit had been a source of food and fur since Norman times. *Conyger*, meaning rabbit warren, occurs frequently as a place name and is no doubt associated with an ancient warren.

The Avon provided abundant fishing and would have added to the diet of the local population.

In 1629 6s. was paid yearly to the lord of the capital manor for the right of fishing in the Avon between Bradford and Barton Bridges. The same sum was paid in c.1660 by Simon Deverell. A fishery in Winsley, Turleigh and Haugh (in Winsley) and Bradford was put in settlement in 1699. (VHCW)

Fishing at Avoncliff.

The period of expansion slowed in the fourteenth and fifteenth centuries and as a result of a series of bad harvests and the plague, populations declined. The Black Death reached Somerset in the autumn of 1348 with catastrophic consequences. Recorded deaths among the clergy at that time imply that the population at large was also devastated. So many died at the Carthusian Priory at Hinton Charterhouse that the brothers asked for labourers to be allowed inside their enclosures to till the land which was lying uncultivated. A survey of the manors of Glastonbury Abbey throughout Somerset, Wiltshire and Dorset show that fifty-five per cent died from the Black Death. No area was unaffected.

Economic recovery from these terrible times was quicker in the Avon valley than elsewhere due to the thriving cloth industry. There was a marked decrease in the cultivation of arable farming and a subsequent increase in sheep-farming. At the same time the great landowners were retreating from direct farming of the demesne land and beginning to lease land to tenants in return for rent money. Land was enclosed and large farms broken up and it was possible in the later Middle Ages for enterprising families to acquire wealth and land. This was exemplified in the Avon valley by the land acquired and the large houses built by the successful wool merchants.

After the Reformation, the greater part of the revenue from tithes remained in the hands of the church but a large proportion was now transferred to the hands of laymen. The seventeenth century saw the beginning of the right to enclose land although this was done somewhat illegally by the dominant landed classes. This proved unacceptable and eventually led to the Tithe Act of 1836 and the Enclosure Act of 1866. The first Act substituted tithes in hand for rent money from landowners and led to a detailed survey of every parish. Large scale maps were prepared, detailing every farm, wood, building and field and providing a valuable record of the state of each parish around 1840. Of particular interest is a well-researched book by Mrs Gee Langdon called *The Year of the Map: Portrait of a Wiltshire Town in 1841*. The book and its map provide a factual background survey in the parish of Bradford on Avon in the 'Hungry Forties'.

Awards under the Enclosure Act gave villagers specific plots of land adjacent to their respective properties in exchange for the traditional grazing rights on common land. In addition the overseers of the poor were given a large piece of land which could be divided up as allotments and specific plots for those villagers with no land of their own. In the case of a village such as Bathford the allotments remain unchanged although the separate plots of land have now been sold for building.

As the wool and cloth industries emerged, sheep farming was of paramount importance. No doubt some sheep grazed in the valley and on the surrounding hills but the necessity to have ever larger flocks for the hugely expanding industry meant that valley farms would keep their sheep many miles away on farms on the downs and the Cotswold hills.

Forestry and the clearance and management of woodland, particularly coppicing, provided a vital resource for building and many other needs. The term coppice comes from the French word *couper* meaning to cut and was first practiced in Neolithic times. When the shoots of native trees are cut close to the ground many new shoots will grow rapidly from the base and the resulting poles can be used in a variety of ways. Alder was used for clogs and scaffold poles and the versatile hazel, which is Wiltshire's main coppice species, was used for thatching spars, making houses out of wattle and daub and above all for hurdles for penning sheep. Coppicing is still practiced today, particularly in nature reserves where the labour-intensive work is often carried out by volunteers. The oak tree was the major source of building material for houses and the bark from the oak was used for tanning. There was a tanning mill at Turleigh.

In Medieval times woodland still covered large areas and the valley was close to three immense forests – Kingswood Forest to the north-west, Bradon Forest to the north-east and the Forest of Selwood to the south. The old Welsh version of the name of Selwood *Coit Mawr*, The Great Wood – was mentioned in 709 when Bishop Aldhelm died. He was known as the 'bishop west of the wood'. Canon Jones, in his remarkable history of Bradford written in 1859, on examination of the Domesday Survey of 1086, writes as follows:

> The meadow and pasture land is reckoned at about four hundred acres: the wood at about one hundred and forty acres. The small amount of the former is perhaps accounted for by the fact of there being in these early times a very large portion of common land unenclosed and uncultivated, which is not included in the Domesdary (sic) reckoning. The latter calculation may relate principally, though not entirely, to what is now called Bradford Wood, and does not include many pieces of woodland and coppice, that even in extent, must formerly have been double that size, by no means an improbable supposition, as, in a survey of 1785 it is described as 'about 105 acres', and within the memory of many now living, parts of it have been grubbed up and tilled. Indeed, nothing is more evident than that in olden times there was a much larger extent of wood-land than now. This is true of comparatively modern days. In a schedule of lands and tenements leased out under the manor in the eighth year of Charles I, hardly more than 200 years ago, there was one tenement described as being in 'Pepitt Street, near Bradford Wood'. The wood alluded to must have come right down almost into the middle of the town.'

It is interesting to see the extent of arable farming in the nineteenth century in comparison with our own time in the parish of Bradford. 'In 1861, 1,237 acres in Bradford parish were sown with wheat, 491 with barley, 438 with oats, 280 with peas, 170 with beans, 100 with potatoes and 85 with turnips.' (VHCW). According to the Tithe Map of 1841 there were fifty-three farms, mainly run by tenant farmers, the most important being Barton Farm. The word 'barton' means 'demesne farm', this being part of the manor. It was let by the Lord of the manor, Sir John Hobhouse, to George Spencer who combined farming with being a coal merchant. His coalyard and adjoining tenement were also rented from the Lord of the manor.

In recent times the valley floor has been used mainly for grazing with only a small proportion given over to arable farming, although more crops are grown on the fertile flat ridge fields. The introduction of a deer farm on the slopes around Claverton has revived an ancient tradition of keeping deer in that particular place. A small amount of forestry is done on the north side of the river near Conkwell where conifers are grown and hewn and where there is active management of the woodland.

Further east along the valley at Murhill there was in the mid-1800s a huge and productive orchard. The *1848 Postal Directory* refers to Murhill as a 'vulgar abbreviation of Summerhill, consisting of 10 cottages, 300 acres of fruit, 25,000 trees – the finest orchard in England if not the world'. Despite the accurate detailing of the 1841 tithe map the orchard here is not clearly marked. In fact the map is remarkable for showing no trees where Murhill woods are today. The orchards would have been below the area of the quarry, reaching right down to the canal. In this century the pro-

Picking grapes at Elms Cross Vineyard.

duction of strawberries is well remembered by residents in Murhill and the strawberry farms contributed much to the life of that part of the valley until about twenty-five years ago.

The history of viniculture has sparse but interesting documentation. Vineyards at Elms Cross near Westwood were mentioned in the Domesday Survey and once again there is a flourishing and expanding wine business here. From small beginnings in 1975, 7,500 vines have now been planted on this ten-acre vineyard, with plans for another 3000. Possibly for the first time, red wine is to be made from Cabernet Sauvignon grapes. These grapes have to be grown under a polythene tunnel as they do not ripen naturally in this climate. In c.1670 John Aubrey's observations, when visiting Bradford, included ideas for a vineyard. Writing of Paul Methuen's property, facing south on the hill above Bradford, he felt 'that part might be turned to better profit, for it is situated as well for a vineyard as any place can be.' Records do not relate if the Methuens took up the idea.

A vineyard did flourish at Claverton and was described in a diary by George Skene who visited Bath in 1729:

> Went on the Common for an airing which is a fine piece of carpet around on the top of rising ground, two miles round where they have a horse course. (Claverton Down race-course - abandoned in 1784 in favour of Lansdown.) Down from this is a Vineyard of six acres of ground where they will make seven or eight hogsheads of red and small white wine which will yield ten pounds a hogshead. They tread the grapes in a trough and then carry them to the press which is like a cider press with the frame and all, only that they put the grapes in the frame which is full of holes in the sides, without any haircloths and squeeze it into another frame - this takes out all the juice. (From *The History of Claverton*).

Vineyard Farm still exists today.

Except for small family vineyards, for example at Crockford Farm and Little Ashley Farm, few grapes are now grown on or near the valley slopes. As more agricultural land is taken out of use this would seem an excellent crop for the sunny south facing valley slopes. However, a recent EC directive has stated that England now has enough vineyards and that any other vines grown must be 'quality' grapes. Please refer to Brussels for more information. Meanwhile the future of agriculture anywhere in Britain is extremely uncertain. The Economic Community requirement to reduce farming all over Europe has thrown the industry into confusion. Farms still abound in this area and the Limpley Stoke Valley will be closely watched for unwanted intrusions by all who love it but at the same time having sympathy with the farmers' dilemma for possible uses of unwanted land.

The following is extracted from the West Wiltshire District Plan (Draft Plan for Deposit) February 1993:

> The District Council recognises that the beauty and diversity of West Wiltshire's countryside depends on a prosperous rural economy. The maintenance of a healthy rural economy is the best way to protect, manage and improve the countryside because much depends upon the investment of people and other resources to maintain the countryside that is West Wiltshire. Additional income is required to supplement farm businesses so that they may continue to manage the country-side in the traditional way, thus maintaining the pastoral landscape and rural scene to which local people have become accustomed.
>
> The District Council recognises the urgent need to address the challenge of diversifying and sustaining the rural economy and the creation of new jobs in the District's rural areas without sacrificing its environmental quality. It is proposed to encourage farm diversification projects, where appropriate, particularly where

this will help maintain the countryside as a traditional landscape.

The District Council accepts the guiding principle that development should benefit the rural economy and maintain or enhance the environment. Thus it will seek to encourage new opportunities for rural employment, in appropriate locations, having regard to the need to protect the special character and appearance of the District's villages, rural areas and wildlife interests.

Agricultural Buildings

The supply of wood, excellent building stone available in and around the valley, and the wealth derived from agriculture and the wool industry, led to the construction of some splendid farm buildings. The remorse of King Offa of Mercia (crowned 758) for the murder of Ethelbert in 792 led him to give all the tithes of his kingdom to the Church. The introduction of tithes into England probably stems from this time although it was not until 1200 that tithes were ordered to be paid to the particular parish in which they arose and the Tithe Barn came into existence. All tithes were paid in kind and remained so until 1841. In the fourteenth century a great and glorious barn was built at Barton Farm, Bradford on Avon, to house the produce gathered as tithes from the surrounding parish.

Tithe Barn, Bradford on Avon.

It is a massive and splendid building constructed, not to the glory of God in thankfulness for his bountiful goodness, but for the wealth of Shaftesbury which was rapidly becoming the richest nunnery in England. As they trundled their produce over the lovely fourteenth century bridge which spans the Avon at Barton Farm did the peasants and serfs and workers of the field in those medieval days wonder at the size, as we now do, of the Tithe Barn?

Although the barn at Barton Farm, and its associated cruck-framed granary nearby, would have housed tithes of corn and hay, it would have been used as a general store for the products of the grange. The Bradford barn is 167 feet in length and 30 feet in width and is divided into fourteen bays with two large porches on the north side and smaller ones on the south. It is only slightly shorter than its sister barn at Tisbury (said to be the longest in England) also belonging to Shaftesbury. The latter has a thatched roof but the stone slates of the Bradford barn are thought to produce a finer building. The addition of the massive weight of the stone roof necessitated the building of an additional buttress in the north wall and props and tie beams were placed in strategic places to counterbalance the spread and thrust of the weaker part of its walls.

Surviving periods of deterioration and decay over the centuries, the barn is now cared for by English Heritage having been extensively renovated by the Ministry of Public Buildings and Works in recent times. Recently, for a short but controversial period, it was leased to house exhibitions of old farm implements and the like. Much wrath was caused locally by the levying of an admission fee to enter the barn. This has been resolved – the barn is now empty and people are free once again to enter the cool interior of this massive, solid and mysterious building which has seen so much life down the ages.

The valley is rich in these particularly well-constructed barns and many early ones survive. Westwood Manor, owned and administered by the National Trust, has a huge, detached barn standing a little distance from the house. The ancient Manor House, church and barn form an integrated scene of great beauty and peace. In the summer of 1992 the barn was used to great effect by the Bradfordians for their production of 'As You Like It' when rain stopped play on the lawn of the Manor.

Winsley Manor also has a massive detached barn and it is still a farm building. However, planning permission has been granted to turn it into a dwelling. This may be an expedient move by the present owners and as yet development of the barn has not begun. Long may it remain as it is.

The great barn at Turleigh has undergone the dreaded 'development' and it is particularly unfortunate in this case. The view from the Bradford to Turleigh road used to be one to be treasured with the ancient farm buildings merging into the hillside as if they were part of the landscape. The development into many separate dwellings has produced a fussy, somewhat messy picture with the added affront of modern Velux windows – quite wrong for a lovely old barn. Fortunately, a recent application for the conversion of another barn in Winsley has been accepted but only with the deletion of the Velux windows. Also in Winsley, Barn House, a converted barn once belonging to the seventeenth century Winsley House Farm, has chapel-like windows and a hidden history.

Among others of note is Claverton Manor Farm from the seventeenth century which had some good outbuildings of the same date. These have now undergone development and although no doubt pleasant to live in, the barn is now unrecognizable as a farm building. Happily other barns survive more or less intact; a notable example is Little Ashley Farm near Winsley. Built of stone with a stone-tiled roof it has integral buildings on each side, the whole structure with its massive wooden door being particularly pleasing.

Dovecote at Monkton Combe.

There is a large, square, sixteenth century dovecote attached to Church Farm at Monkton Combe and above the village, up on the hill Combe Grove Farm is, according to Pevsner, a late Georgian house with good early nineteenth century outbuildings. Belcombe Court, between Turleigh and Bradford, has a series of courtyards one of which has a massive fifteenth century barn and stables. Freshford also has some interesting old stables with 'Gothick blank quatrefoils' from the late eighteenth century (Pevsner).

One of the oldest surviving barns in the area is found in Bradford on Avon. When Priory Barn was built in 1460 it was part of a large estate on the north edge of the town. Two hundred years after the original house and barn were built, it was owned by the Methuen family and known locally until the beginning of this century as The Methwins. The barn has survived the house which was tragically pulled down in 1938 leaving only the high wall in Market Street and fragments in the grounds. This late medieval barn with its splendid roof timbers and slate roof once held a commanding position on the hillside which, according to Aubrey when he visited in the seventeenth century, was covered by elders. 'At Bradford all the side of the high hill, which faces south, above Mr. Paul Methwins' house, is covered with them.' Today one would be forgiven for not realising that the building was or had been a barn as it is now part of the street which runs through Newtown. It is owned by the Bradford on Avon Preservation Trust and used for lectures and exhibitions.

West Wiltshire District Council Policy on the Conversion of Rural Buildings is as follows:

The conversion of rural buildings in villages or the open countryside to residential use will normally be permitted provided that:-

A The building is in sound condition and capable of conversion without extensive alteration, rebuilding, and/or extension or otherwise significantly altering its original character.

B The proposed conversion safeguards and/or enhances the essential form, structure, character and important traditional features of the building and the countryside .

C The proposed conversion does not conflict with the objectives and the preservation of the Western Wiltshire Green Belt.

The Woollen Trade

Every now and then the great sixteenth century chronicler Leland throws us crumbs of tantalizing historical information. When he visited Bradford in c.1540 he made two often quoted remarks describing it as 'made all of stone' and that 'All the town of Bradford stondith by cloth-making'. Indeed the little town built all of stone was a thriving, prosperous and important centre for the woollen industry, its many fulling mills dotting the River Avon and its tributaries, particularly the River Frome, all the way to Bath and beyond to Bristol.

Until the mechanization of the fulling process in the fourteenth century, the most important centre in the West Country for the cloth industry was Bristol. Fulling or 'tucking' as it was known, is the process of cleansing, shrinking and felting the cloth by beating and washing. Originally this was done by trampling the cloth with the feet in a trough, pressing it between rollers and cleaning with soap or Fullers Earth. The water-driven fulling mill was now able to mechanize these labours by connecting water-wheels to a series of cogs which lifted and dropped wooden hammers to pound the water from the cloth. The earliest of these machines, which in many cases replaced, or at least shared the space for, the grinding of corn, first appeared in records in the Cotswolds in 1185.

The industry settled wherever water-power was available and the fast-flowing Avon and its tributaries were ideal. Between the fourteenth and nineteenth centuries, the process by which wool is made into cloth, and the trade that was associated with it, had an enormous influence on life in the area. The mills spread quickly down the valleys and effectively relocated the industry from towns to rural villages along the river valley where weirs and millstreams were created to drive the water-wheels. On the Avon from Bradford to Bath and as far as Bristol, up the River Frome, the By Brook and Midford Brook, evidence of fulling mills can still be found. Old decaying wheels, rusting machinery, ivy-covered buildings, water still rushing past ruined walls, all point to an industrial past that brought wealth and prosperity for centuries.

Decaying mill at Avoncliff

Most of the famous names that echo down the centuries were part of that industry, names such as Horton, Yerbury, Methuen, Houlton, Druce, Ashe and others. Associated with these names are the splendid buildings constructed of local stone, a manifestation of the great wealth derived from wool. Thomas Horton, the best known and the first of the great clothiers from the Bradford /

Westwood area, added a chapel to the parish church at Bradford and made some wonderful additions to the Manor House at Westwood. He also spent time and money altering the church at Westwood. In the eighteenth century Yerbury persuaded John Wood the Elder to forsake the building of Bath for a while to redesign part of Belcombe Court. After its construction Wood felt Belcombe to be one of his finest achievements. Leland describes Bradford's finest mansion, The Hall, situated close by the Avon, as 'the best house for the quality of a gentleman in Wilts'. Although not in the immediate area a mention should be given of Corsham Court built by the Methuens who materially improved the wool trade in Bradford by introducing weavers from Holland in 1659 'for the purpose of obtaining, through them, the secrets of manufacturing the finer kinds of cloth.' (Canon Jones: *Bradford on Avon*). The unique manor houses of Great Chalfield and South Wraxall are also worthy of note, being built by the great clothiers of the time.

All over the West Country the opportunities afforded by the woollen trade were exploited to the full. This was a time of increasing population, rising prices and far-reaching changes in rural society. Guilds were set up for the protection and mutual aid of the workers. There was great expansion of markets and fairs, a great fair being held annually at Norton St. Philip, as well as numerous smaller ones. From the earliest time wool dominated the lives of most people and continued to do so until the 1820s when it went into decline.

The woollen cloth industry in the area fell into two distinct categories. The first, beginning around 1300 until about 1610, involved workers with the necessary skills of spinning, weaving and fulling in the production of a white or undyed broadcloth which was sent to London to be finished and dyed abroad. During the first half of the seventeenth century James I tried to monopolize the broadcloth trade by attempting to have all cloth dyed and finished in England. The scheme failed and had disastrous consequences for the West County, particularly in Wiltshire. Despite a consequent slump in the trade and much unemployment the clothiers managed to diversify and adapt their skills. During the second and later phase of the trade, a new coloured cloth called 'medleys' was woven and sold for the home market as well as abroad. This was developed largely through the efforts of the Methuen and Yerbury families, whose inspiration to import Flemish workers to provide expertise in the new enterprise, made Bradford the centre of this new industry, achieving fame and prosperity for another three hundred years. A visit to the Bath Costume Museum provides marvellous examples of the quality of the locally woven and finished cloth.

The majority of the work in the industry was carried out in the villages up and down the valleys. In the seventeenth and eighteenth centuries the town houses, such as the tiered ranks above Newtown in Bradford were for skilled workers employed in the finishing processes of the cloth. It was a time of industrial pollution with noise night and day from the fulling stocks, the smell of urine and lanolin used for the fulling process, the latter causing froth in the streams and rivers and the further pollution of the rivers when dyeing the cloth was part of the process. This would have been particularly bad in the By Brook where upstream at Castle Combe the famous red and white cloth named after that village was supplied for soldiers overseas for a period of twenty-two years. The red dye would no doubt have tracked downstream as far as the Avon.

This was an industry which employed more women than men; women, and their children, who sat for long, long hours spinning in their homes, (hence the term 'spinster'). Even in the factories in the nineteenth century women outnumbered the men. In 1816 Dunkirk Mill at Freshford employed nineteen men and fifty-seven women. By 1800 there were thirty-two factories in Bradford and the population swelled to ten thousand. The problems engendered by the factory system and the introduction of new machinery in 1791 prompted a riot as workers feared unemployment. The introduction of scribbling machines and the ensuing troubles culminated in three deaths. This was the subject of an ambitious and extremely well-received community play in 1990 called 'Under the Fish and Over the Water', performed in a Bradford school with many local inhabitants acting in it or becoming involved in some way.

Dunkirk Mill, Freshford, as it is today.

Much has been written about the West of England cloth industry and local libraries have many books and references on the subject. There is therefore little need to elaborate any further here. Two books particularly worth a mention are *Wool and Water, Bradford on Avon and the River Frome* by Kenneth G. Ponting and *Wiltshire and Somerset Woollen Mills* by Kenneth Rogers.

The Stone Industry

There is no better way to appreciate the labours of the stone quarry workers than to tour one of the now defunct mines in the area. Monks Park near Corsham not only provides an insight into the activities of those superhuman men but also a geology lesson within the primeval depths of the earth's crust.

It was on such a visit that my imagination took flight. As we descended eighty feet into the dark abyss of a stone mine, I experienced a feeling of returning to the womb of nature. On our way down we passed through two hundred million years of the evolution of our earth in the formation of these beds of oolitic limestone. This process had begun in Jurassic times with fragments of broken shell and grains of sand which, over millions of years, had rolled around in the seas becoming coated with lime, gradually becoming compressed into beds of oolitic limestone. After the slow northward drift of Europe, the tilting of the limestone beds of Britain formed an outcrop of fine building stone laid in a diagonal band from Purbeck in the south to the Yorkshire Moors in the north.

Erosion of the land surface ultimately created the Avon Valley, cutting through the southeast sloping sequence of rocks and making it relatively easy for man to mine the stone two hundred million years after its conception. Then came the men who could, with a pick, shovel and saw, chavel out great pieces of this superb freestone, to carve and sculpt and create some of the most beautiful and noble buildings in the world.

Prehistoric man built enclosures for his cattle and walls for his dwellings with the stone found on or near the surface of the land. He learnt the rudiments of dry stone walling, an art still practised today. Aerial photography has detected boundary lines and walls built by the Celts, now fallen and buried under an accumulation of earth. Some remain on the surface, notably the standing stones on Bathampton Down which mark ancient boundaries. Celtic field systems also are evident on Bathampton Down and on the flat land east of Warleigh Woods at Farleigh Wick. Iron Age earthworks at Hayes Woods near Freshford reveal the quarrying of stone and again, in later centuries, by the Romans. There is also some evidence of Neolithic and Bronze Age barrows in the area. In 1944 J.P.E. Fal-coner published his 'Flints on the Bath Downs' describing a barrow found on Claverton Down.

Two thousand years ago the Romans quarried stone mainly from outcrops and shallow surface workings. Stone from Box Hill was used to build the large, ornate villa at Box. Combe Down, and possibly Box, is thought to have been the source of stone for the baths and Temple of Minerva and other prestigious buildings in the valley below.

As the baths fell into disrepair the Saxon builders took advantage of the ready-made blocks and in 781 built St. Peter's Abbey known to be of 'wondrous workmanship'. In the sixteenth century this was replaced by the present Abbey using some of the stone hewn long before by the Romans. This has been the general practice throughout Britain down the ages leaving us with only the ruins of that ancient culture.

The discovery of the famous Box Ground Stone by the Saxons was recorded by Aubrey in the seventeenth century. The traditional story is that St Aldhelm, riding across Hazelbury near Box, threw down his glove and 'bid them dig there and they should find great treasure' – meaning the stone beds. The stone was used for the building of Malmesbury Abbey by St Aldhelm – who is also thought to have built Bradford's Saxon church. The stone from Hazelbury was ideally suited to the building of other great religious houses in the area including the Priory at Monkton Farleigh and the Abbey at Lacock.

Working on site cutting stone, 1987.

Bath Stone, as it is often called, is a vague and misleading term as it covers stone produced from quarries from Bath to Corsham. In each quarry the quality of the stone varies greatly and can differ in appearance and durability. Stone taken from one quarry, when tested scientifically, can show many textures and variables, a problem which could not be ignored by the builders through the centuries. The Golden Age of Bath stone arrived with the rebuilding of Bath in the eighteenth and nineteenth centuries. The valley also bristles with magnificent residences, many attributed to the famous Bath architects with the name of Wood, particularly those around Bathford.

But the remarkable flowering of English architecture at this time must not overshadow the achievements of the medieval builders. Up and down the valley great manor houses were constructed of local stone. Money derived from the woollen trade produced wonderfully durable buildings of great beauty. To name a few: the Manor House and Manor Farm in Winsley, Westwood Manor and Turleigh House all date from the sixteenth or seventeenth centuries or earlier. Burghope House in Winsley and Avonside in Limpley Stoke all have Elizabethan features. In Monkton Combe the Monks Retreat near the church dates from the fifteenth century and there are lesser buildings of ancient origin, many built for the weavers. Sheltering below the rampart of Farleigh Hungerford Castle is a little thatched stone house which has stood beside a freshwater spring near the River Frome from the fourteenth century.

Limpley Stoke has weavers' dwellings and cottages in Middle Stoke dating back to at least 1550. The forerunner to the Hope Pole Inn, a monks' wine house, could have stood in 1300 AD. The present building dates from 1580. There are other notable ancient stone inns around the valley, particularly those at Freshford and Westwood. The two great Tudor Manor houses of Claverton and Warleigh have been replaced by other splendid buildings, the latter a Tudor revival built in the early nineteenth century and described by Pevsner as 'a picturesque Tudor villa with Victorian additions'. The present Claverton Manor, now the American Museum, is an imposing mansion built by Sir Jeffry Wyattville in the eighteenth century, who had, unfortunately, persuaded the owner of the old Manor House to pull it down and build anew.

The stone from the Hazelbury Quarries, and to a lesser extent at Bradford, provided most of the material for the needs of the medieval builder. After 1600, and particularly in the eighteenth and nineteenth centuries, great quantities of stone were used and many quarries opened in the area. A map produced in 1895 by *The Builder* shows the stone-producing districts and quarries at that time. In an area encompassing Bath, Corsham, Westwood and Bradford there were nine districts providing work for men in forty-eight mines and quarries. The hillsides are honeycombed with underground passages and caverns hewn out of the rock by men who were not paid unless they produced a perfect block of building stone.

One of the most important engineering works requiring massive amounts of stone was the construction of the Kennet and Avon Canal between 1793 and 1810, including its many stone bridges and two huge aqueducts. At Westwood, Murhill, Conkwell and Dry Arch specially designed trolleyways from the quarries to the canal transported the stone. After the completion of the canal these same trolleyways were used to load the stone onto barges for transport to other parts of the country, providing material for the building of anything from Oxford colleges to the Palace of Westminster.

One other industry connected with stone quarrying was the limestone roofing tile which enhances so many of the buildings in this area and beyond. Within the Forest Marble clays which occur locally there is a thinly bedded shelly limestone which splits easily into slabs. The quarried stone was left in the open for the winter and the frost did the work. A prime example of its use is the great Tithe Barn at Bradford.

Today only two mines near the valley, at Limpley Stoke and Westwood, are producing stone. Recently, the latter supplied the stone for the cladding of the new library in Bradford. The passages and caverns of other mines have had uses varying from munitions storage to mushroom farming with some becoming tourist attractions. Open quarry faces and underground passages are invitations for exploration but there is a warning that entry into any one of them can be dangerous, besides often being on private land. To gain more understanding of the geology of the valley and the workings of a mine, a visit to Monks Park or Westwood is highly recommended. Comparing the old methods with the new is possible at the Bath Stone Company's Stoke Hill Mine at Limpley Stoke which has recently re-opened and where the latest technology and mining methods are employed.

West Wiltshire District Plan - Wiltshire Minerals Local Plan

Planning applications for chalk, clay and stone working will be considered against the need for the mineral and the potential environmental impact on the local area. Proposals for new workings and extensions to existing workings within an Area of Outstanding Natural Beauty or Special Landscape Area will be subject to rigorous examination. Proposals within AONBs will normally be approved only when there is a compelling National or Regional need which is greater than the need to conserve the environment, character and natural beauty of these areas in the national interest.

The Brewing Trade and Valley Inns

The traditional industries of malting and brewing provided employment throughout the region. The beginning of the seventeenth century saw an increase in hop growing, particularly in the south where the chalklands provided the barley for malt. Such was the desire to consume large quantities of beer, farmers in the Avon valley would have no doubt provided space for this particular crop and indeed we have seen that in 1841, 491 acres in the parish of Bradford had been sown with barley. By the nineteenth century brewing was a thriving industry, the chief centre being in Berkshire where fortunes were made and the population increased as unemployed labourers were drawn to the area.

Small-scale brewing took place in the villages and farms along the Limpley Stoke Valley and whether through habit or because of the dark days of the collapse of the woollen trade, consumption per head was enormous. In the nineteenth century, Bradford had four malthouses that served nineteen public houses. The Newtown Brewery and Malthouse, known as the Seven Stars, operated until the First World War. The impressive though dilapidated buildings have recently undergone renovation and are being sold as flats and offices.

There was a brewery with malthouse at Winsley and others at Turleigh, Freshford and Limpley Stoke. Bathford had at least two principal breweries one of which, the Woodside Brewery, brewed and sold beer in great quantities to quarrymen until 1865 when it became a beer-house known as The Quarrymen's Arms. While Brunel's Box tunnel was being constructed for the G.W.R. many hundreds of itinerant rail workers were housed in Bathford, Box and Corsham where according to the 1928 GWR Magazine drunkenness and fighting were carried on to an alarming extent. Some 26 inspectors were employed, supervising the work on the railway generally and a number of these men were sent to different villages to keep the peace on Sundays, or at any rate as well as they could, there being no County Police at that time.

Many of the ancient village inns are still thriving, notably the Hop Pole in Limpley Stoke where the hop plant still grows near the pub. Most of the building dates from 1580 but has possible connections with Hinton Priory as far back as the thirteenth century when a monks' wine lodge may have stood on the same site, the remains of which make up part of the back of the present inn. The sixteenth century Inn at Freshford stands beside the fourteenth century bridge over the Frome, and The Inn at Westwood, the Wheelwright at Monkton Combe, the Cross Guns at Avoncliff and the Seven Stars at Winsley have all contributed and continue to do so, to the social life of the valley. The Rose and Crown on the main road at Limpley Stoke began as a beer and cider house and gradually changed to a 'house selling cider'. When the new Warminster Road opened in the 1830s it served teas to weary travellers. Although the name Rose and Crown was given to the earliest public houses to celebrate the end of the Wars of the Roses, the building is likely to be of seventeenth century origin. It stands above the old Hydropathic Spa Establishment (now the Limpley Stoke Hotel) and enjoys superb views up and down the Avon valley.

The Hop Pole Inn, Limpley Stoke.

Houses built close to the canal during its construction sometimes have connections with the brewing trade. Elbow Cottage, close to the bridge over the canal near Freshford, was built in 1810 as an alehouse which sold ale but, unlike the inns, did not provide accommodation. The Dagger family lived on the hill above the pub at Murhill. Ernie Dagger, who died some thirty years ago, used to repeat stories told him by his grandfather and greatgrandfather who had been quarrymen. There was a cock-fighting pit at Elbow pub which was greatly patronised by the coal miners of Radstock who came as the crow flies over the hills to attend the fights. In case of a police raid they would only have to cross back over the river to be in a different county where the police would not follow. Canal Cottage nearby at Murhill may not have sold ale but an early photograph uses this idyllic spot to advertise Somerset cider! The orchards near the house may well have produced cider to be sold locally.

Bathford's Crown Inn near the bridge over the By Brook is known to have been in existence in 1757 when meetings of the Turnpike Trust took place here. It was substantially rebuilt in 1904. The oldest inn in Bathford stands at the top of Bathford Hill, the old turnpike road to London. In 1733 it was known as the New Inn. In 1755 it was conveyed to a new owner under the name of the Old Inn. By 1832 it had become the New Inn again and is known today as The Inn. Two previous inns in Bathford are now private residences. The Star Inn, which alternated with the name The Rising Sun, closed its doors in 1957. The Smith's Arms which started life as a smithy and began selling beer in 1866, became two private residences in the 1930s.

7   Transport

As has been seen, Bath was an important centre from the time of the Romans
with roads radiating out in all directions. For a thousand years Bradford on Avon
had been an equally important link in the local system of communications. But
until comparatively recent times there was no direct connection through the valley between the two towns. This is the more surprising as the Limpley Stoke
Valley now stands as a monument to the innovative transport systems of the
eighteenth and nineteenth centuries.

The route of any transport system is largely determined by the physical
landscape through which it runs. For centuries the fast-flowing Avon and its
steep wooded hillsides prevented the creation of an effective route. But in the
eighteenth century it was the river itself which provided the water for the Kennet
and Avon Canal which for forty years was a link between Bath and Bradford
bringing growth and prosperity, and pleasure to passengers who journeyed on
the canal amid wonderful scenery. In time the railway took its place. It was not
until the 1830s that the main road from Bath to Warminster (the A36) was cut
through the valley, linking up with the existing Bradford Road (the B3108) at the
Midford Viaduct.

Early Roads, Trackways and Bridges

From the time that Early Man forged trackways through the previously impe-
netrable forest, inhabitants of the valley have, through the centuries, added to
the network of pathways, lanes and minor roads linking the villages and settlements. Early bridges occur at Barton Farm where the fourteenth century packhorse bridge spans the Avon, and another comfortable, solid stone bridge of the
same date crosses the Frome at Freshford. Between Barton Bridge and Bathford
there was no crossing for vehicles until Stokeford Bridge was built at Limpley
Stoke in 1751. As the names suggest, the river was forded at Bathford and
Stokeford. There is little evidence that the bridge at Bathford existed before the
thirteenth or fourteenth century, although Bathford owes its origin and continued existence as an important junction from Roman times. Indeed, in the
eighteenth century the only route to Bath from London was through Bathford.
The Turnpike Act of 1707, calling for the improvement of roads out of Bath, placed
great emphasis on the first five miles between Bath and the top of Kingsdown.

This Act was one of the earliest in the country and was renewed again for further improvements around Bathford in 1720 and 1739.

The ancient ford over the By Brook on the west side of Bathford Bridge was used until recent times. The site of the ford over the Avon is a little upstream, close to the site of a Roman villa:

> The route from the ford over the River Avon went straight up through the field known as Horselands, up Court Lane, crossed Pump Lane and continued in a south-easterly direction possibly originally to the Romano-British settlement at Inwoods. No record of a date when this ford ceased to be in use has yet been found but H.D. Skrine states this to have been about 1800. Subsequently a ferry took its place and was in use certainly in the 1860s.   (G. Laurence: *Bathford Past and Present*)

The ferry crossing, with its steps and slabs of stone either side of the river, is found just below Warleigh Weir. The original ferry boat was wrecked during a flood and its replacement in 1952 was reported locally:

> A proud and sturdy craft called the *Queen Mary* has made her maiden voyage – no massive liner this, just a small flat-bottomed boat with as captain, George Moulder, ferryman at Warleigh. At the launch ceremony was William Treble who had been ferryman for twenty-two years before George Moulder took over. The boat belongs to Miss A.D.M. Skrine who named it *Queen Mary* because she was the only Queen to have visited Warleigh.

The ferry service was discontinued some years ago although Ferry Cottage still exists on the hillside above.

The names Stokeford and Crockford in the vicinity of the bridge at Limpley Stoke, suggest there was a crossing here, perhaps dating from Roman times, but of little more than a series of stepping stones. Later there was a rickety wooden footbridge which was replaced in 1751. The new Stokeford bridge was built of four stone pillars providing three arches and with a wooden frame.

Besides the smaller minor roads which connect the various villages around the valley and date from medieval times, the valley is full of ancient trackways and much loved footpaths. They frequently lead from the hillside villages to the river and canal. Walks in the valley are a delight. The numerous flights of mossy stone steps in Limpley Stoke, the tracks in the woods around Conkwell or the ancient holy well called Shingle Bell in the middle of ancient Pucklewood, are all there to be discovered by the inquisitive rambler.

The first Road Act for Bradford was passed in 1752 and a Turnpike Trust was set up for the repair of the road that ran from Combe Bridge (Somerset) via Winsley to Bradford. In 1777 the Act was renewed and provision made for the upkeep of the Avon Bridge at Limpley Stoke (VHCW). Much to the disgust of local people, tolls had been taken on the bridge from 1773. The gate house, which still stands near the bridge, was built in 1841 when the gate had its own tariffs:

> For every wagon, coach, chariot or other
> four-wheeled carriage, one shilling.
> For every cart, chaise or other
> two-wheeled carriage, sixpence.
> For every horse or other beast, one penny.
> For every score of sheep, lambs or pigs,
> five-pence.
> For every ox, cow or other neat cattle,
> one halfpenny.
> For every foot passenger, one halfpenny.

With the increase in traffic the old bridge was weakened and a new stone structure was completed in 1858, providing three inlets for pedestrians to stand while traffic passed. In 1930 and again in 1964 the bridge was strengthened and doubled in width. The inlets are still much used by pedestrians to shout advice to fishermen below!

Bridge at Limpley Stoke.

The improvements to the road would undoubtedly have included the widening and reconditioning of Winsley and Brassknocker Hills. Even so their steepness must have been a daunting prospect for coaches and wagons, particularly on Brassknocker. It was not until the 1830s that the viaduct across the Midford Brook was built, with its eleven arches said to have taken only two 'hard working' months to build. A tremendous amount of rock was excavated to take the road up Stoke Hill towards Warminster. The route to Bath along the valley also presented difficulties being frequently flooded by the Avon.

In 1792 the road from Bradford via Bathford to Bath, known today as the Bath Road, became a turnpike. It was completed in 1795. The section through Warleigh Wood became known as the Sally-in-the-Woods road. Sally is known variously as 'the widow of a Warleigh Manor game-keeper who lived in a cottage just below the new road and lived to a great age', a 'steam engine that carried stone from Monkton Farleigh to Bradford' and 'the errant wife of Wade Brown who went hunting in the woods'.

It would be interesting to hear the definitive version!

By 1822-3 there were coaches from Bradford to Bath every day except Sunday and a wagon service daily to Bath. In 1830, the daily run was undertaken by two coaches, the *New Regulator* and the *Accommodator*.

Valley Roads in the 1990s

One hundred and fifty years after the coaches between Bath and Bradford were proudly travelling on the new turnpikes, no new roads have been built in or close to the valley (except for two-thirds of a bypass around Winsley). True that the A36 and the A363 have been surfaced, improved and widened in places but the motor car, not invented until this century, now travels on roads built for horse-drawn vehicles. It was not surprising then that tremendous pressure has been brought to bear to improve the road system, particularly around Bath and Bradford.

The storm clouds gathered and in 1988 the *Bath Chronicle* published a shattering picture on its front page of a drawing of a motorway running straight down the Limpley Stoke Valley. The warning bell was ringing loud and clear, alerting the valley to potential disaster and giving birth to BRAVE – The Bath Region and Avon Valley Environment Group led by the inspired and tireless Brian Coombes. For a couple of years proposals for new roads in or near the valley were put forward by the Department of Transport. Concerned groups of people – Parish Councils, Preservation Trusts, Traffic Action Groups and others – had numerous meetings and sleepless nights. Eventually the final proposals were presented at a Public Inquiry – a motorway would not be built but a road linking the A36 with new roads around Batheaston and Swainswick would cross the valley from the meadows near Bathampton Bridge to feed into the A36 at the Dry Arch. To many thousands of people the link road was unacceptable as the impact on the valley environment would be devastating. The Public Inquiry took place in Bath in 1990 and lasted seventy-five days ending on December 5th. The Inspector,

Sir Michael Giddings, reached his decision in June 1992.

All objectors had been fully informed throughout the proceedings and were sent a copy of the decision letter of the Secretaries of State for the Environment and for Transport. In it was a summary of the Inspector's conclusions and recommendation; he concluded emphatically and without any reservation against the case for the A36 Link, considering it to be 'unimpressive in trunk road terms, prejudicial in some important respects, intolerable in its landscape impact and devastating to recreational amenity.'

It was a historic day of victory for the valley but joy was tempered by the further threat to Bradford on Avon. The building of the Swainswick Bypass without the Link would engender ever more traffic through the town. Proposals for widening and improving the A363 to dual traffic purposes standard between Bath and Beckington, including a bypass around Bradford and running close to Bathford, are being discussed. If this is the favoured route it will not be built until the next century. Perhaps by then the oil will have run out and we can reintroduce the horsedrawn *New Regulator* and *Accommodator*.

The Kennet and Avon Canal

The river, railway and canal are all such familiar features, snaking their way through the valley, mainly running parallel with each other, that it is strange to think of the valley without the latter two. However, before the middle of the eighteenth century, a navigable waterway from Bristol to London, was a mere dream. The railway was still a century away.

A vital ingredient for the prosperity of Bath was to provide an easy method of transport downstream to Bristol and back. John Wood planned and built the Avon Navigation between Bath and Hanham, where the water became tidal, thus providing communication by water between the two towns and allowing the architectural development of Bath to take place. It was opened in 1727. The River Kennet Navigation from Reading to Newbury Wharf had opened in 1723 and there was an obvious need to link Newbury with Bath, thus providing a waterway to link the Thames and the Avon across southern England.

The idea of using the River Avon above Bath as a navigable waterway was explored by Ferdinando Stratford in 1765 but was found to be unworkable. A canal was chosen in preference, despite the immense geological and engineering difficulties that were sure to follow.

John Rennie completed his survey of the canal in 1793 and work began on the first section between Dundas and Bath in 1794. This was complete by 1800. Despite a shortage of good building stone for the two aqueducts, problems with land slippage on the section between Avoncliff and Limpley Stoke, and the necessity of building twenty-nine locks at Caen hill near Devizes, the canal was officially opened in 1810. The aqueducts and the Pumping Station at Claverton have provided the valley with three outstanding features which still inspire awe and wonder. In recent years the old and crumbling stone of the huge aqueducts which carry the canal high over the railway and river at Dundas and Avoncliff have been made watertight during restoration of this part of the canal. The superb machinery and waterworks at Claverton have been lovingly restored by dedicated volunteers and can be seen in working order on various days of the year.

The story of the canal and its recent history and restoration has been well documented and will not be repeated here as there are numerous, excellent books on the subject. The rebirth of the canal has been the biggest and most exciting project in the valley since the coming of the railway which had spelt its demise in the nineteenth century. Apart from its obvious attractions for leisure and pleasure, it is the ideal educational material for children and beloved of primary school teachers in villages all round the valley. A walk along the towpath, demonstrations of the workings of a lock, a visit to the marina or pumping station, discusssing the construction of the canal, climbing aboard a barge and looking for wildlife on the water and the banks – all these are compulsory activities for lucky, local children.

Barge on Kennet and Avon Canal below Murhill.

The student of industrial archaeology could do a complete study on the trolleyways which connected the quarries with the canal. Rails from the inclined trolleyway running at Murhill can still be seen on the hillside. This quarry and trolleyway opened in 1803 to supply stone for building the canal. Murhill wharf, long buried in tangled undergrowth, was rediscovered during renovation of the canal. It is now relatively clear of brambles and nettles and once again a barge is moored to its walls. The face of the quarry is now scarcely visible buried in the woods at Murhill, woods which did not exist in 1803. It was operated throughout the first half of the nineteenth century by James Berber, a Fellow of the Geological Society of London, who advertised the quarry to be let in 1857. In fact the stone was of poor quality, as evidenced by the crumbling faces of Avoncliff aqueduct.

At the far end of the valley the arch spanning the Warminster Road and known as Dry Arch was demolished in recent times. Stone was brought down from the quarries on the downs above, across the stone arch and down to Hampton Wharf on the canal. The line of the tramroad in the field below Dry Arch can still be seen. Other tramroads, or trolleyways, were at Conkwell, Avoncliff and Limpley Stoke each with its own wharf on the canal. The quarried stone was used either in the construction of the canal or sold further afield after its completion. In this century, a resident of Limpley Stoke remembered small trucks filled with stone rumbling down the steep incline to the stone yard beside the station. Here the stone was cut and loaded onto the railway for transportation.

The most interesting example of industrial archaeology from the nineteenth century is Claverton Pumping Station. At the western end of the canal at Bath, the canal drops to the river by means of a flight of six locks. Each time a boat passes through this flight thousands of gallons of water are lost to the river. In 1810 John Rennie devised a way of replacing this water by siting a pumping station at Claverton which was capable of raising up to ten thousand gallons an hour from the river into the canal 14 metres above it. The river itself drives the massive waterwheel inside the pumphouse. For 140 years water was transferred this way until in 1952 a log became trapped in the wheel causing some of the wooden teeth on the 4.9 metre 'pit wheel' to be torn off. The pumphouse was acquired by the Kennet and Avon Canal Trust in 1969 when the long job of restoration began. Once again in full working order, it is frequently open to the public throughout the summer season, although it is not now used for transferring water to the canal. This is done by a modern pump nearby.

During the building of the canal an Act of 1796 was granted stating that 'the position of Dundas aqueduct to be seven furlongs below Limpley Stoke, instead of above as originally planned'. It is hard to imagine John Rennie siting his aqueduct anywhere else but at Dundas, where it is the focal point of this beautiful area. Dundas Wharf with its proximity to the A36, attracts growing numbers of visitors to its glorious setting high above the Avon and where sufficient artefacts remain to feed the imagination. Its junction with the coal canal, the brightly coloured narrow boats moored in the basin, the woods climbing up the hillsides, the little cluster of buildings and its fascinating history are all enhanced by the grandeur of the stone structure which leaps across the valley, at one with its environment.

Similarly the same Act required a variation in the location of Avoncliff aqueduct: 'The position of Avoncliff aqueduct to be below Avon Mills, instead of above as originally planned.' Although it is another glory of the valley, this aqueduct has fared less well than its neighbour down river at Dundas. The stone has crumbled and leaks have been frequent. When the railway was brought through the valley it was necessary to burrow into the hill beside the aqueduct and the resulting tunnel was built of brick. Repairs to the face of the aqueduct have also been done in brick. The narrowness of the towpath and deep drop to the water in the aqueduct has apparently necessitated the use of an incongruous modern railing. Despite being able to walk, cycle and boat to this lovely area, discussions on the pros and cons of more parking space continue to rage and must be resisted. Car parks bring more traffic. If access is known to be difficult, Avoncliff might survive a little longer as a haven of natural beauty and peace. Already, with the introduction of stark, white, terraced walls and the ugly, green, undisguised sewage tank in the grounds of the Cross Guns Inn, together with the ever-growing popularity of this beautiful place, Avoncliff is under threat of being ruined.

The story of the renovation of the canal in the valley is one of hard work, lack of funds, land slippage, frustration and ultimate triumph with the grand opening of the canal by the Queen at Devizes in the summer of 1990. More frustration was to follow with four years of drought preventing the use of the flight of locks at Devizes. More land slippage between Bradford and Avoncliff has meant further re-lining of the canal. Work has also been needed on the stretch between Dundas and Claverton.

Despite setbacks the canal is a jewel in the valley's crown; a waterway which provides hours of gentle activity along one of its most beautiful stretches. It must not be spoilt by over use. The marinas at Bradford and Trowbridge are, on the whole, an asset but if they are allowed to expand too much the resulting boat traffic will surely clog and ruin the waterway for everyone. It must be shared for all types of recreation. At the Boat Show at Earl's Court in 1992, Year 200 celebrated two centuries of inland waterways as well as introducing a new barge with a blunt-nosed bow which effectively cuts down the bow wave which can lead to erosion of the banks and disturbance of wild life along the water's edge. However, there is still a particular plea from fishermen for boatsmen to keep to the speed limit of four knots. Another request is to avoid a proliferation of 'nature trails' and such like. Nature is there for all to see – it should be discovered, not pointed out.

The Somersetshire Coal Canal

On April 17th, 1794 the following Act was passed:

> An Act for making and maintaining a Navigable Canal, with certain Rail Ways, and Stone Roads, from several collieries, in the county of Somerset, to communicate with the intended Kennet and Avon Canal, in the Parish of Bradford, in the County of Wiltshire.

On the same day both the Kennet and Avon Canal Act and the Somersetshire Coal Canal Act received the Royal Assent.

One can only feel sympathy and some sadness for those great canal enthusiasts of the eighteenth century. Despite overcoming unusual and often frustrating problems with the building of the Somersetshire Coal Canal, it prospered for only a short time and is now little more than a derelict ditch – a history lesson for the industrial archaeologist. At least the Kennet and Avon Canal has survived to see another heyday.

However, for half a century or more barges carrying coal from the Somerset coalfields negotiated the narrow waterway down the Midford Valley, including the flight of twenty-two locks at Combe Hay which replaced the aborted Caisson Lock, to bring prosperity to the area. The Kennet and Avon Canal also prospered greatly from its connection with the SCC and initially half the tonnage carried on its barges was accounted for by coal.

In time, and with a certain inevitability about it, the railways brought about the demise of both canals. The Kennet and Avon Canal was the first to suffer despite a last ditch flurry of intense activity to overcome the competition from the steam train. But it was to no avail and eventually the Canal Company bowed its head to its arch-rival and sold its rights to the Great Western Railway in 1852.

Entrance to Somersetshire Coal Canal.

In 1898 the SCC was to suffer a similar fate but, whereas the Kennet and Avon Canal continued and survived as a canal under Great Western Railway ownership until the 1950s, no buyer could be found for the Coal Canal. In 1904 an Act confirmed that the canal had been abandoned and was derelict and this opened the way for sale to the GWR. By 1907 work started on the Camerton and Limpley Stoke Railway along its bed.

Now, at the end of the twentieth century, almost like a restored object for inclusion in a museum, the section of the SCC between the A36 and Dundas Wharf has been brought back to life. Sadly, the little stone hump-backed bridge at the entrance to the canal has long gone. It has been replaced by an aluminium lift-bridge. After much careful restoration, the Coal Canal is again navigable as far as its junction with the A36 and is used by the Bath and Dundas Canal Company for mooring narrow-beamed pleasure craft. Frustratingly, this small, restored section is prohibited to all except hirers and birth-holders but glimpses of the boats bedecked with flowers, canal paintings and bunting can be seen from across the valley from the Kennet and Avon towpath, or from the B3108 near the Viaduct.

Dundas Aqueduct carrying the Kennet and Avon Canal across the River Avon, and the hump bridge over the Somerset Coal Canal, from an old print.

The Great Western Railway

The coming of the railways had a huge impact on the valley and the surrounding area. Besides the obvious advantage of fast and reliable transport, the construction and operation of the railways brought much needed employment at a time when hunger and poverty were at crisis levels. It created wealth by opening up previously unimaginable markets in far flung places. Industries, such as agriculture, market gardening and coal, had much to gain.

The first line from London to Bristol, built by the Great Western Railway Company, ran just north of Bathford, en route to Bath. The greatest obstacle to its construction was 99 miles from Paddington - Box Hill, through which Brunel built his famous tunnel. It was described in an article in the Great Western Railway Magazine for 1928 as 'this range of elevated ground lying directly between and about equidistant from Chippenham to Bath. It comprises several strata of oolite stone and Fuller's earth ... and yields vast quantities of stone'. Three hundred horses were used and up to four thousand men at one time were employed in building the tunnel which was started in 1836 and opened on June 30th, 1841. During that time a hundred men were killed in different parts of the works and a large number injured. On the day of opening 'a decorated train with flags left Paddington at 8 a.m. and is reported to have reached Bristol in four hours. The first train, however, to use the new piece of line between Chippenham and Bath left Bristol at 7 a.m. for London'. Bathford Halt was not opened until 1929 and continued in use until 1965.

Curving away from the River Avon and joining the London route at Bathampton is the Salisbury/Westbury/Bath route which was constructed between 1857/8 and runs beside the river on its west side down the length of the Limpley Stoke Valley. At Dundas it passes under the aqueduct and continues to Freshford where the meandering Avon is joined by the Frome River at which point it is carried over the river by a low, six-arch bridge. Having passed under the aqueduct at Avoncliff, it returns to the west side of the river at Bradford on Avon.

Originally the line was a single track but by the 1880s a second track was laid on the whole of the Westbury line. Despite the railway running through their town, much to the annoyance of Bradford people their station was not built for another ten years. There was a station at Limpley Stoke which closed in 1965 and now the only existing halts between Bath and Bradford are Freshford and Avoncliff.

Despite the obvious convenience of the railway, its intrusion into the valley, the noise of the trains and the ugliness of the railway line was abhorrent to many people. The updated (1907) version of Canon Jones' book on Bradford, which he wrote in 1850, describes one of the principal events of his time:

> The construction of the railway from Bath to Salisbury, involving that of the unnecessarily hideous bridge over the Avon close to the beautiful old Barton Bridge, to the great detriment of the scenery.

Derelict Station at Limpley Stoke.

Pasture land was used and houses in Limpley Stoke were demolished to make way for the railway which severed the lovely gardens bordering the peaceful Avon, causing much distress. For most residents though, the railway was extremely popular, providing exciting and easy transport to Bath and Trowbridge by steam train. The station at Limpley Stoke grew in importance and its yard, which is now the Hop Pole Inn car park, received vast quantities of coarse limestone from the quarries above. It was brought on trollies, down the original canal tramway, part of which is now Woods Hill, and stacked in the yard awaiting transportation on the railway waggons. The huge blocks of stone, which became popular as a good hiding place for children, were sawn up in the yard before being lifted by two small cranes. The dust and the noise of the sawing is well remembered by residents.

More and more sidings were laid near the station. At the beginning of this century, just before the Great War, the station received large quantities of coal from the Somerset Coalfields, via the new Camerton to Limpley Stoke line. During the First World War the sidings were used for hospital trains from Southampton which would wait overnight before taking wounded soldiers to hospitals in Bath and Bristol.

Despite the great affection people had for 'the puffers', by the 1930s buses and cars were preferred as a means of transport. By the 1960s the station was scarcely used and it closed in 1965. The line is now used by diesel, sprinter trains and goods trains carrying aggregate from the Shepton Mallet quarries. On Sundays, because of mainline maintenance, the Intercity 125 London train is diverted to the line through the valley. Pride of place is taken by the Orient Express which runs a special side-trip from London, through the valley, to Bath, its distinctive brown and white coaches looking somewhat out of place. Go to Bath Station on a Wednesday or Sunday afternoon and watch the spectacle of wealthy Japanese being photographed with the Orient Express as a backdrop, before jumping aboard to continue their journey across Europe!

The Camerton and Limpley Stoke Railway

In 1904, an Act authorised the abandonment of the Somerset Coal Canal and it was duly bought by the GWR for £20,000. In 1907 work started on the new railway, between Camerton and Dunkerton collieries, before marking out the course of the proposed Camerton to Limpley Stoke line. The completed railway, which in part used the bed of the old canal through the Midford Valley, was opened in 1910 and filtered into the main line where the Midford Brook joins the Avon.

Initially, five passenger trains ran daily between Limpley Stoke and Hallatrow on the single track line. There was a halt at Monkton Combe, with sidings at Limpley Stoke and Hallatrow, the train taking thirty-two minutes to travel the route at a cost of 11d single fare. Three or four goods trains, carrying coal from the collieries and other goods ran daily until Dunkerton and then Priston collieries were closed in the 1920s. Camerton colliery closed in 1950. Monkton Combe Public School and the Royal Mail helped keep the line open but it eventually had to close to all traffic in 1951.

Two films were made using Monkton Combe and the valley as a backdrop. The first was 'The Ghost Train' made in the 1930s. The second film, made in the 1950s, provided a certain poignancy. As Dr Beeching's axe fell on many lines and rural stations, the sadness and anger had already been brought to life in the film 'The Titfield Thunderbolt'. Dr Beeching either cannot have seen the film (now a classic) or chose to ignore it for it tells the story of a village that loses its railway and, as a result, the villagers try to run it themselves. The station chosen for the film was Monkton Combe. Freshford became Titfield Village with many local people taking part. The 1938 train used for the film was taken out of mothballs from the Railway Museum in Liverpool and during filming it was kept at night in a siding at Limpley Stoke.

8　Tributaries of the Avon

The Valley of the Frome

The History of the West of England cloth trade could be written as the economic history of this river valley.
(K.G.Ponting: *A History of the West of England Cloth Industry, 1957*)

The River Frome, a tributary of the Avon, has its source in the Mendips and flows north. It should not be confused with the River Frome that has its source in the Cotswolds and flows south to the Avon at Bristol. Today, the peace of this delightful river valley belies its extraordinary history. Tempting though it is to venture as far as Tellisford, Rode and beyond to explore the medieval migration of the textile industry along the Frome, the stopping point will be Farleigh Hungerford in Somerset.

The river emerges from its deeply incised and wooded valley to join the Avon in the fields below Freshford. With the Wiltshire village of Westwood on the ridge to the east, the Frome and the village of Freshford have their being in Avon (which used to be Somerset). Two miles up river at Iford, the line of the county boundary actually passes through the Manor House and then hugs the river for a few hundred yards before veering off to the east and returning to the Frome at Stowford. South of Iford weir, three counties meet as the borders of Avon and Somerset merge with Wiltshire to the north.

The Romans discovered the Frome and occupied the hills on either side of the valley near Iford where traces of settlement have been found. The Domesday Book records Iford under the name of *Eford* as comprising fifty acres and two cottages on the Wiltshire side of the river. It was included in the large tracts of land around Farleigh Castle and held by Count Morton, brother of William the Conqueror, showing it to be an area of some importance in the eleventh century. Iford was leased to a Saxon known as Alured and his neighbour across the river was Count Devereux who held the Iford land on the Avon (Somerset) side. By the thirteenth century the Carthusian monks at Hinton Priory had taken possession and here they built a mill and probably constructed the old stone bridge in about 1400 A.D. The original ford is discernible downstream from the bridge.

The castle at Farleigh Hungerford was built between 1369 and 1383 by

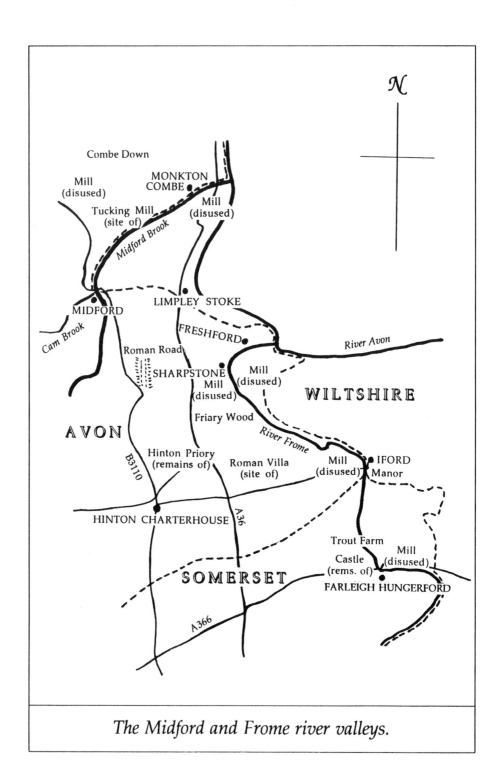

The Midford and Frome river valleys.

Sir Thomas Hungerford, a Wiltshire squire who was Speaker of the House of Commons in 1377. Except for two ruined towers, exposed foundations, a very impressive gatehouse and a chapel built in 1425, it relies for its romantic aspect on its colourful history and its superb position above the river. At various times through the summer the Company of Chivalry brings the past to life at Farleigh Castle. Members of the Society, which reconstructs military and civil life as it was around the year 1370, wear medieval costume and take on roles in the households of two rival knights, challenging each other to contests in a tournament. It is an ideal way to learn about Farleigh's complex history.

*Sir Thomas Hungerford
in stained glass in
Farleigh Hungerford Church.*

The foundations of the massive tower walls are buried deep in the grass-covered ditch and nestling below in the shadow of the huge mound is a tiny, thatched fourteenth century cottage, still standing beside a gushing spring. In the 1860s the natural springs gave rise to watercress beds and it was here that a Mrs Bishop ran a successful tea garden for many years, complete with water garden and stream. Now the spring, which produces one and a half million gallons of water every day, fills the tanks of a flourishing trout farm. Nearby on an island between the mill stream and the River Frome a fulling mill was in operation in 1548. It was the last country mill to close down and was worked until 1910.

In 1369, as the castle grew from its foundations, the mill at Iford was, until 1686, part of the Farleigh Hungerford estate and was leased to a succession of great names in the cloth industry. The Horton family, John Yerbury and Paul Methuen were among the clothiers who, through the centuries, found this mill on the Frome irresistible. Most of the existing two-storey stone building dates from the sixteenth or seventeenth centuries and it remained a cloth mill until 1850 when it was converted for grinding corn. Water from the mill stream still rushes under the building which is now a private residence. Nearby is the 'Archers Field' used as a training ground for bowmen, a requirement from the period preceding the Battle of Agincourt. In the orchard on the opposite bank, amongst carpets of snowdrops which are replaced by daffodils in spring, are the remains of a couple of weavers' cottages.

It was while John Horton was working Iford Mill in about 1480 that the existing Manor House was built and further extended a century later by John's nephew

Thomas Horton. Meanwhile John's son, another Thomas, was busy up the road extending Westwood Manor, now owned by The National Trust. The classical front at Iford was added in the eighteenth century by William Chandler and it was at the end of that century that the garden, particularly the woodland walks, started to take shape under the visionary eye of the Gaisford family. In 1899, Harold Peto, an architect and associate of Sir Edward Lutyens, bought Iford and designed the garden we see today. It became the setting for his splendid collection of antiques and much of his design was influenced by the charm of old Italian gardens. His ideas, which combined architecture and plants, produced a unique assemblage of steps, terraces, streams, pools, statues, colonnades and delightful buildings such as The Cloisters. The eighteenth century statue of Britannia on the bridge, which was donated to the County of Somerset, was also Peto's inspiration.

Further downstream, where Friary Wood climbs the hillside to the south, a small stream gurgles down the open meadow and passes through a small settlement known as Friary, once owned by Hinton Priory and used as quarters for the lay brothers.

On a bend in the river near Freshford, Dunkirk Factory and Freshford Mill stand on opposite banks. Freshford Mill is found below the weir where the water was easily harnessed from the fast-flowing river and like the numerous mills upstream contributed to the enormous growth of the local cloth industry. In the early centuries the fulling mill was the property of Hinton Priory. By 1545 it had been sold and passed to various owners, including the Freshford clothier John Ashe who made a fortune from the newly introduced medley cloths, and the well-known Methuen family. In the nineteenth century it was extended as a factory with '20 scribbling and carding engines with room for billies and jennies. There was also a dye-house and stove and a millman's house'. By 1816 this thriving mill and factory em-

Britannia on the bridge at Iford.

ployed ninety-two people and presented an industrial scene which would have been an environmentalist's nightmare. The nearby fields were draped with cloth being stretched on wooden and iron tenter racks. Washing-bridges to wash the scouring substances from the wool were erected and the wool suspended in running water in perforated containers. The smell of urine used for scouring, lanolin from the wool and the dye from the dye houses, here and further upstream, polluted the river as it ran past buildings which rattled and vibrated with the noise of machinery working all day and most of the night.

Variously altered, with many modern additions, the extent of the original building is unclear. In 1945 the mill was bought by the Peradin Rubber Company who, until recently, traded here under the name of Peradin Bonded Polymers. Where were the planners when the modern additions to the factory were built? Who allowed the hideous sprawl of industrial building to spread over the entrance to this beautiful valley?

On the opposite hillside, a spring and a stream, rather than the river, have contributed to the life of Dunkirk Factory. In 1733 it consisted of 'four tenements, a stove, a mill-house formerly a tucking mill and malt mill and two large fish-ponds at Pond House'. The mill itself had disappeared by 1792 but a factory at Dunkirk was certainly in existence by 1795. In 1816 it employed nineteen men and fifty-seven women who produced '30 cloths a week'. A thirty-two-foot water wheel was installed inside the mill and turned in winter by the stream nearby. This was probably removed in 1856 when a forty horse-power steam engine was installed. The life of the mill ended in 1912 when it was sold. The building fell into disrepair and for years stood as a spectacular ruin as the roof fell in and ivy enveloped the entire structure. In the 1980s it was carefully restored and converted into flats.

Pond House still stands on the hillside above, its lawns and gardens enhanced by the tumbling stream which issues from the woods above. Below the house, and just above Dunkirk Mill, are a series of tanks and ponds filled by the stream and used by the Avon Tributaries Fishing Club to rear trout for stocking the Frome.

The last mile of the Frome before its junction with the Avon is as delightful as any part of its journey from the eastern limits of the Mendip Hills. Fish lurk in the shallows under the humped-back bridge near The Inn at Freshford. Dippers, grey wagtails and kingfishers inhabit its banks and fish in waters now relatively clear of the industrial pollution that the river endured for so long.

The Midford Valley

The tributary that feeds the Avon to the south of Combe Down runs through a river valley that, like its sister tributary the Frome, bears the marks of a long and varied history. Once again water has played a major part in its bustling industry but dependence on the geology and landscape have produced a very different picture from that in the adjacent Frome valley.

Two smaller tributaries converge at Midford to become the Midford Brook. The Cam rises in the foothills of the Mendips to the west of Bath and Wellow Brook has its source in the eastern Mendips south of Radstock. The enlarged Midford Brook meanders through the fertile valley and is joined by the Horsecombe Brook at Tucking Mill before merging with the Avon near Monkton Combe. The deep valley is flanked by steep slopes which rise five hundred feet to the north and three hundred and fifty feet to the south. Between Midford and the River Avon, the Brook is the boundary between the County of Avon to the north and a spur of land that is Wiltshire to the south. It is as beautiful as the valley of the Frome.

The valley is a secret place, a place of rocks, ancient woodlands, leafy lanes and water. The past is seen in remnants of the abandoned canal and railways, the stone quarries on Combe Down, the derelict De Montalt Mill below the Down, Monkton Combe Mill and the history that abounds around Tucking Mill. The present age is one of farming, wildlife and water. All have been, and are, dependent on the geology of the valley, the secrets of which began to be unravelled in the eighteenth century by the pioneer geologist William Smith.

If William Smith is remembered for little else he should go down in history as the man who was employed as a temporary 'plumber' by Bath City Council. In 1810 the hot springs suddenly failed and Smith, a well known geologist, was called in to help. Much to everyone's dismay he insisted on opening the spring at its source, revealing that it had found an alternative channel. He restored the flow to its original course and the people of Bath, whose livelihood depended on the waters, heaved a sigh of relief.

William Smith.

Of more relevance to the valley, this self-made geologist was appointed Resident Engineer to the Somerset Coal Canal Company in 1795 and helped in the planning and building of the Coal Canal, linking the coal pits in North Somerset to the then partially completed Kennet and Avon Canal.

William Smith was born in Churchill, Oxfordshire in 1769 where his father was blacksmith and his grandparents and great grandparents were farmers. William's father died when the boy was eight and he lived with his uncle who encouraged his interest in fossils. At eighteen, after a meagre education – a fact that he regretted all his life – he was employed by Edward Webb, a local surveyor, and travelled extensively with him. At the age of twenty-two he was sent by Webb to do an underground survey of coal mines near High Littleton in Somerset. His interest in geology inspired him to observe the unusual rock formations in the area and he realised they were similar to those in Worcestershire. Later he wrote 'my subterranean survey of these coal views, with sections which I drew of the strata sunk through in the pit, confirmed my notions of some regularity in their formation'.

Whilst employed by the Coal Company from 1794 to 1799, Smith became familiar with the strata through which the canal was to pass. He collected fossils and recognised that the assemblage of types could be related to certain strata and that there was a regular occurrence exposed in different areas of the country. He listed the rock layers in a 'Table of Strata near Bath' and began drawing coloured maps to show the different beds outcropping around the neighbouring hills. In 1799 he had identified enough of the strata to produce a coloured geological map of a five mile radius around Bath which is held by the Geological Society of London. He went on to produce the first geological map of England and Wales on a scale of five miles to the inch.

While working for the Canal Company, Smith purchased Tucking Mill in the Midford Valley. He also acquired a quarry on Combe Down and stone was conveyed on a specially constructed railway to the Mill below. This was sawn into blocks and transported along the coal canal which was only yards from the house. Unfortunately the stone was of poor quality and led to Smith's eventual financial ruin. But his years in the valley were happy and he owned Tucking Mill House for twenty years. It was his favourite home and later in life he wrote some nostalgic verse about it.

I made the woodman's axe resound
The oaks were levelled to the ground
The thorn and briar cracke'd on the fire
and Goodly ground was cleared
And fruits and garden shrubs appeared.
Great Plans were laid, a fish pond made
Combining taste with trade
That wandering path which leads to Bath
Contrived to ease the hill
And Freestone Blocks torn from the rocks
Run down to yonder mill.
O Tucking Mill I love thee still
And oft afar in fancy trace
My musings there beneath thy bower
'Tis contemplation's place...

In 1799 the Canal Company terminated Smith's employment. This was thought to be due largely to his criticism of the ill-fated Caisson lock built by the Company at Combe Hay. Here, on private property, are preserved the principal remains of the different attempts to overcome the hundred foot difference in levels between the beginning of the Somerset Coal Canal and its junction with the Kennet and Avon Canal. While Smith was Surveyor for the Canal Company, attempts were made to overcome this change in levels by a new invention called a Caisson – a gigantic watertight box in which boats could be raised and lowered about fifty feet in one operation. The Caisson lock was the invention of Robert Weldon who may have got his basic idea from Charles Darwin's amazing grandfather Erasmus Darwin. Erasmus can be regarded as the innovator of the vertical canal lift and he described the principle on which the lift functioned:

> Let a wooden box be constructed so large as to receive a loaded boat. Let the box be joined to the end of the upper canal and then the boat is admitted and the doors of admission secured again. The box with the boat in it, being balanced on wheels or levers, is let down and becomes part of the inferior lock.

Darwin had envisaged counterweights rather than complete submersion in a water-filled cistern which Weldon eventually built. On June 9th, 1798, the *Bath Herald* described 'the dimension of the Lock, the Stone Cistern being 81 feet long, 20 feet wide and 61 feet deep and the Wooden Caisson being 80 feet long, 10 feet wide and 11 feet high'. At first the lift worked well and early trials were greeted with great enthusiasm. However, the cistern began to leak and Smith felt this was due to the Lower Fuller's Earth clay in which the cistern was excavated. The clay changed volume by absorbing water thereby exerting alarming pressure on the walls causing them to bulge and leak. Eventually the whole project was abandoned. It is sugggested that Smith's anti-Caisson lobby led to his dismissal. He would have realised from his geological knowledge that the Caisson would have been unsuitably sited in Fuller's Earth and presumably said so.

Though he still owned Tucking Mill, Smith left the area and spent some time on the construction of sea defences on the east coast of England before various coal-mining projects took him to Yorkshire and Lancashire. His fame spread and after the publication of his geological map called *A Delineation of the Strata of England & Wales, with part of Scotland* he was known as 'Strata Smith'. Eventually, financial difficulties forced him to sell Tucking Mill and he spent the last twenty years of his life in Yorkshire enjoying the recognition of his work and, as he called it, 'versifying geology':

> *Theories that have the earth eroded*
> *May all with safety be exploded*
> *For of the Deluge we have data*
> *Shells in plenty mark the strata,*

And though we know not yet awhile
What made them range, what made them pile,
Yet this one thing full well we know -
How to find them ordered so.   *Dated Nov.26, 1829*

In 1974 Joan M. Eyles, an authority on Smith, published her research indicating that the tablet erected on Tucking Mill Cottage in the Midford Valley is not Smith's house. The real Tucking Mill (now known as Tucking Mill House) is situated fifty yards along the road. The cottage is still wrongly marked. This tablet was originally erected in 1888 on the mill adjoining the cottage and when the mill was demolished in 1931, it was transferred to the cottage itself. The evidence presented by Joan Eyles was based on land tax returns which reveal changes in ownership. Also a pencil sketch done by Smith and found among his papers confirms that the tall, narrow building could not represent Tucking Mill Cottage but is consistent with Tucking Mill House in its original form.

Tucking Mill

Although Tucking Mill House and Cottage remain, the mill, as noted above, was demolished in 1931. It stood on the banks of the canal next to the cottage on the left of the Wessex Water Authority entrance and had been a fulling mill, using the nearby Fuller's Earth to scour and thicken the wool producing a heavy felted cloth. Behind the building, a millpond powered the waterwheel. The pond was enlarged by Smith and he installed mechancial saws to dress the stone from

Tucking Mill (artist's impression).

his quarry on the hill above before transportation by barge along the canal.

In 1886 the millpond was drained and replaced by a new Fuller's Earth works. Beneath the hard limestone cap which tops the downs surrounding Bath, is a layer of Fuller's Earth clay. This easily eroded deposit, which has been responsible for the slippages and 'cambering' of the limestone, was used for centuries by mill owners in the fulling process. The Avon Wildlife Trust's Tucking Mill Trail Guide describes the mining process:

> Clay was mined at the top of Horsecombe Vale and taken by tramway to the bottom of the valley beside Horsecombe Brook. Here it was crushed and mixed with water, and sent down a pipe alongside the brook to the works. The slurry was poured into pools and after the clay had finally settled the water was drawn off. A works boiler house circulated hot air through drying sheds. Dried Fuller's Earth was finally loaded into sacks and taken by wagons to Bath for export by rail. In later years the mineral was employed in a new way in the oil refining process in the U.S.A.
>
> The works closed down after World War Two. The 80-foot boiler house chimney remained standing until its demolition in 1968 and ten years later the remaining buildings were completely removed to make way for the most recent phase in this site's history.

High on the hill above, springs give rise to Horsecombe Brook which descends the Vale to join the river at Tucking Mill. In 1881 a waterwheel pump returned the water to an elevated tank at Combe Down as part of the public water supply system. Later, a coal steam engine and then gas replaced the water power. An exceptional drought in 1976 called for radical measures and the newly formed Wessex Water Authority filled the valley of the Horsecombe Brook with a reservoir as an impure water storage lake. Strangely, the reservoir is not filled by the stream above but by the Avon, one and a half miles away, where submersion pumps lift the water to the reservoir through large-bore pipes. Horsecombe Brook itself is culverted under the lake and the road. Various experimental treatments are being tried by the adjacent Wessex Water Research Station to assess the efficiency of extracting impurities from the water.

With a backdrop of mature beech and hornbeam and fringed with lakeside plants the reservoir is delightfully situated. In 1981, the Year of the Disabled, fishing rights were established for disabled anglers who share the lake with the resident wildlife – chaffinch, moorhen, coot and kingfisher. The lake is stocked with carp, roach and tench. Across the valley to the north of the lake is an eight-arch viaduct which carried a single line from Bath to Evercreech Junction. This was the Somerset and Dorset Railway, beloved of John Betjeman, which opened in 1874 carrying coal from the Mendips to Bath through the Combe Down tunnel, the longest unventilated tunnel in Britain. Passengers who used the single line steam train from Bath's Green Park Station to Evercreech Junction, had a great affection for the S and D which was known either as the 'Slow and Dirty' or 'Swift and Delightful'. The line was axed by Dr Beeching in 1966.

An exposure in the railway cutting near the viaduct reveals beds of limestone lying on soft sandstone. These are the Midford Sands, the oldest rock in the area, which underlies the fossil rich Inferior Oolite limestone. The lowest layers of the limestone contain thick-shelled bivalves, especially *Trigonia* which are found worldwide, as well as brachiopods, ammonites, belemnites and gastropod shells. The upper layers of limestone here belong to the Upper Coral Bed and contain mounds of the coral *Isastrea* which developed in warm tropical sunlight filtering through the shallow sea that covered the area 170 million years ago.

Other Mills in the Midford Valley

Beside the river below Monkton Combe School stand several one and two-storeyed stone buildings. These, and the brick chimney stack nearby, probably date from the later nineteenth century but in 1771 a grist mill stood on the same site and was let to a baker from Weston, near Bath. In c.1794 it was bought by Philip Shrapnell, a clothier, (and member of the family who invented the lethal casing for shells for firearms) when it became a fulling mill and remained so until 1809 when it was converted to a factory by a clothier called Richard Whittington. Fame and fortune did not fall on this Richard Whittington as he went bankrupt in 1815. Little is known of the mill until the Freeman family ran it as a flock mill between 1875 and the 1940s. It is now used as a retail store.

Further up the valley a mill of a different kind was built by the De Montalt family in 1805. The family had inherited Ralph Allen's estate and their mansion, mill and cottages for the mill workers all stand on the slopes of Horsecombe Vale below Summer Lane. Springs, at the junction of the limestone and Fuller's Earth clay, fed a large mill pond which powered a fifty-six foot water-wheel for the mill which produced high quality paper until about 1834. Thereafter the building was used as a laundry and then for producing natural rubber.

Above the mill on the down, the stone quarries, probably worked as opencast mines by the Romans, had their heyday in the eighteenth and nineteenth centuries when they were owned and worked by Ralph Allen for the building of Georgian Bath. The underground quarries extended into the hillside until there were approximately twenty four sites in one square mile. Now subsidence, connected with these underground tunnels, is causing problems for residents who live today on Combe Down.

The woods, meadow pasture, flowers and trees which fill this delightful valley, are described in the chapter on Natural History. Despite being managed and shaped by man, the natural beauty of the two tributary valleys, together with the valley of the Avon, remain relatively unchallanged, yet man's ability to change and spoil, chiefly with the introduction of roads and traffic, is an ever present threat.

9 The Villages

The five valley villages and their associated hamlets are thriving and each possesses a unique characteristic and history which will be emphasised in the following pages. Descriptions of the churches and other village features can be found elsewhere in the book. Writing about other people's villages is a hazardous occupation. Space is provided for only a brief description of each village and inevitably elements will be omitted and errors will occur. For this I apologise and would urge readers to encourage amateur historians to write and publish full accounts of their particular village. This has already been done in the case of Bathford and Claverton, although the latter needs to be up-dated. Elderly residents have a wealth of knowledge and memories. I urge them to start writing.

Bathford

Bathford, 'a village still, not yet a suburb of Bath' (Pevsner, 1958), stands behind its ancient limestone walls at the western end of the Limpley Stoke Valley in the County of Avon, close to the confluence of the By Brook and the Avon. It is the third largest parish in the vicinity of Bath and, if equally shared, each of its eighteen hundred inhabitants would enjoy one of its eighteen hundred acres. In 1791 the Rev. John Collinson estimated the population to be 460 and refers to Bathford as a town:

> The situation of the town is exceedingly pleasant, being on an eminence at the western declivity of the point of a bold hill, called Farley Down, which rises behind it to the height of nearly 700 feet and is so diversified with wild rocks, stone quarries, and irregular patches of wood, as to form a very picturesque effect.

Despite its proximity to Bath, the A4 to London and the A363 to Bradford on Avon, Bathford remains intact, its community close-knit but welcoming. Extensive housing development has taken place in the recent past, particularly in the Dovers Park, Mountain Wood and Meadow Park estates. Soon, the long awaited by-pass to be built in the Bathampton meadows for quick access to and from Bath will bring advantages and disadvantages to Bathford and it may be hard to withstand the pressure of further development in a village which will be particularly attractive to commuters. However, the inclusion of Bathford in the Cotswold Area of Outstanding Natural Beauty will certainly limit development of the surrounding area and also in the older parts of the village which are designated a Conservation Area.

Former Bathford Post Office, closed December 1993, but reopened elsewhere.

More of a threat to the village is the Department of Transport's suggested route for the A36 Bathford-Beckington bypass. Starting at Bathford, at the bottom of Sally-in-the-Wood, the new road would first run below the existing A363 and then cross it and run higher up the slope of Home Wood. Here it would cut into the hillside, then cross and re-cross the A363 using very little of the existing road before by-passing Bradford on Avon. This is one of many alternative routes to link the south coast with the M4 and the north and the growing lobby of anti road-building protaganists will no doubt see this particular route as being extremely destructive to the West Wiltshire countryside.

Roadbuilding around Bathford has been part of life for its inhabitants throughout history. In Roman times both the Fosse Way and the *Via Julia* were within its boundaries, and in the valley the ancient ford across the River Avon went in a direct line up the hill towards Monkton Farleigh. It was the ford that gave Bathford its name. In Saxon times and in the Domesday survey of 1086, it was known as *Forde*. By 1575 a map of Somerset by Saxton has the name Bathford, just as *Hampton* became Bathampton and *Easton* became Batheaston. The name of Forde was still used until the eighteenth century.

Standing as it does in the angle of two river valleys it was the obvious place for the meeting of two main railways lines which were built in the nineteenth century. From its position on the hill it has fine views of the By Brook and Avon valleys, Little Solsbury Hill to the north and distant Lansdown above the City of Bath to the south. Like the other valley villages, throughout history it has been essentially a farming community. When Forde received its charter in A.D. 957, 'ten farms in the place which by tradition of the elders is called Forde' were granted to the monastery of St. Peter in Bath and the monks of Bath continued to hold these farms until the dissolution of the monasteries in the sixteenth century. This charter included the boundaries of land which encircles the three tithings of Forde, Warleigh and Shockerwick. The parish of Bathford today still consists of these three rural divisions.

Bathford is rich in huge and splendid mansions, not least the three Manor Houses belonging to the three separate tithings. The imposing Bathford Manor House was built in the 1770s for the Tynedale family who had previously resided in the equally splendid Bathford House built by John Tynedale in 1686. This latter house was destroyed by fire in 1913 and the present house is a conversion of the stable block of the old Bathford House. A member of this family was William Tynedale, one of the great leaders of the Reformation and famous for his translation of the New Testament into English, for which heresy he was burnt at the stake in 1536.

In 1798 Eleazer Pickwick acquired Bathford Manor House from the Tynedale family. Eleazer, who eventually became a wealthy landlord of The White Hart in Bath, seemed undeterred by his rather inauspicious start in life. It is said that a lady driving through Wick found a baby under a hedge. She took him home and named him Pickwick, having picked him up in Wick! Eleazer became the operator of a successful stage-coach business between Bath and London. Seeing the proprietor's name on the side of one of these coaches, Charles Dickens, delighting in the name, created his immortal Mr. Pickwick.

The Pickwicks and members of the family continued their association with Bathford until 1933. The Manor House and its land was sold in 1887 and after various changes of ownership was purchased by Bathavon Rural District Council who converted the house into flats and developed the land.

The manor of Shockerwick had originally been the place of an open air court which was held near a boundary stone under an oak tree. The court had the ancient name of 'soke' from which Shockerwick may have derived. Adam de Sockerwick held this court in the reign of Henry the Second and built the first house on the site. Shockerwick House today is a nursing home and is the only Grade I listed building in the parish, although there is now some doubt that the beautiful Palladian house was designed by John Wood as originally thought. It was built in the late eighteenth century for Walter Wiltshire, a prominent citizen of Bath and three times its mayor. He had a successful carrier business and at one time transported Thomas Gainsborough's paintings safely and without charge to their destinations. Gainsborough was living in Bath at the time and became a friend of Walter Wiltshire, presenting him with some of his paintings, one of which, 'Orpin, the Parish Clerk' (of Bradford on Avon fame), now hangs in the Tate Gallery.

William Pitt also visited Shockerwick while he was Prime Minister and there learnt of the defeat of Austerlitz by Napoleon. Never quite recovering from the news he died two months later.

The name of Skrine first appears in the Court Rolls of Forde in 1446 and the family name has been synonymous with Warleigh until Miss Anna Skrine died in 1956. The manor of Warleigh became the seat of the Skrine family in 1635. It was bought by Thomas and Henry Skrine for £2,700 apparently from money obtained by Richard, one of Thomas Skrine's sons who found favour at the court of Philip of Spain. The present house at Warleigh was built by Henry Skrine (1788-1853), replacing the original Tudor house which stood to the south. His son, Henry Duncan Skrine, wrote local history books on Bathford and also financed the rebuilding of the church. During this century Sir Winston Churchill attended a garden party at the Manor before making his first public speech at Claverton. After Anna Skrine died in 1956 the house was occupied by Rodbourne College and for some years became a school. It is now owned by Rehabilitation Group Ltd.

Warleigh Manor.

Deep within the hill above Bathford are the honeycombed passages of what was once the parish's most important asset – its now defunct stone quarry. The oolite freestone was worked very profitably for more than two hundred years, the stone from the quarry going to the wharf on Bathford Hill by horse and waggon and then by truck to a siding near Box. In 1936 the Royal Engineers carried out a survey of the vast area of tunnels and, after substantial alterations, pronounced it suitable as an ammunition depot during the Second World War. In recent times the tunnels, with their ordnance storage facilities, became a tourist attraction.

As the quarries declined the mill in the valley prospered. Domesday recorded the presence of a mill on the By Brook. For centuries it was used solely for milling but during the Middle Ages it became a grist and fulling mill. In 1733 it was advertised for sale as a corn and cloth mill 'with a dye-house and a house fit for a clothier'. It was bought by Arnold Townsend who, while clearing an ashbed close to the mill, discovered a water spring found to be full of minerals. Residents of Bathford tried the water and found it provided cures for various illnesses, whereupon the spring was given the title of Bathford Spaw. The famous Dr. William Oliver, physician and founder of the General Hospital in Bath in 1738 (now known as the Royal National Hospital for Rheumatic Diseases), bought Bathford Mill and the house which he used as an occasional residence.

Towards the end of the eighteenth century it was operated as a leather mill and then converted to a paper mill. Known variously as Trevarno Paper Mill, The Bath Paper Mills and, by 1913, The Bathford Paper Mills, it has now settled down as Portals (Bathford) Ltd. and specialises in the production of quality, high-security, watermarked paper for such things as bank warrants and passports. Its hundred and twenty employees are mainly from Bathford and surrounding villages.

Freshford

On a sunny June afternoon in 1993, the melodic, harmonious tones of a brass ensemble wafted across the valley from a garden near the station in Freshford. It was the afternoon of the Freshford Arts Music and Gardens Festival and nine village residents had opened their garden gates to musicians and the public. The sounds of cellos, pianos, clarinets, drums, keyboards, choirs and tenors carried on the air fragrant with roses and honeysuckle. Cream teas were served on lawns surrounded by all the delights of an English country garden.

Amateur gardeners and musicians, both achieving professional standards, abound in and around Freshford and with typical enthusiasm and energy were raising money to fund their village's latest project – the purchase and restoration of the Old Bakery near the church. When complete, as it surely will be, despite the large sums of money involved, the building will be used as an extension to the church for meetings, fellowship and worship.

The project typifies the community spirit found in Freshford. This is the community that financed the building of a large and splendid Memorial Hall which is in constant use; a community where self-sufficiency is part of its heritage. In the past the automony of the village included the running of its own hospital and even its own small fire engine, owned by the village, manned by a crew who received beer as payment, and housed in a shed on Church Hill. The old door in the wall is still there. The fire engine was sold in the 1920s for £2; Freshford residents would dearly love to know where it is now.

As in the past, the life of the church is still much in evidence. Prayers are frequently said for the young people of Freshford who are scattered around the world as missionaries – in Japan, Africa and Moscow, and in our own cities, particularly Liverpool. They return to St. Peter's from time to time and speak eloquently of their work amongst the world's poor.

Collinson, in his *History of Antiquities of the County of Somerset*, wrote in 1791:

Freshford is a considerable parish ... situated on a southern declivity of a hill in a part of the country well cultivated and rendered picturesque and romantick by a pleasing intermixture of hills, woods, glens and deep vallies.

Nikolaus Pevsner, who did not often wax lyrical about an individual village, wrote in 1958:

Freshford is a charming village in a bend of the Frome with the church on top and streets descending to the N.E. and S.E. and the wooded banks on the other side of the river to the N. and to the S.

Here, where the Frome has its confluence with the Avon, Freshford lies in the County of Avon with Wiltshire to the north, west and east. With its associated hamlet of Sharpstone it is covered by Green Belt, the Cotswold Area of Outstanding Natural Beauty and Area of High Ecological Value. For centuries the ancient village was part of North Somerset. When, in 1974, the village was wrenched from its beloved county to be part of the newly formed County of Avon the villagers held a funeral service to mourn their loss. A commemorative tree and stone marks the spot near the county boundary where the funeral took place. There is now every likelihood that the county boundaries will be changed again and the people of Freshford had better prepare for a resurrection.

Civilization in or near Freshford started in 1500 B.C. with a small agricultural enclosure in Hayes Wood south of the Warminster Road. Later developed by the Romans, who may also have used the site as a quarry for buildings in Bath, Hayes Wood still stands in its agricultural setting, its physical aspect little changed since its ancient beginnings. Just north of Peipard's Farm and close to Hayes

Wood, the outlines of the deserted village of Woodwick, which had close associations with Freshford, can still be detected on aerial survey photos. In Collinson's day, Shaston (now known as Sharpstone) lay half a mile south of Freshford and contained six houses. One mile south was an outlying hamlet known as Shrubs (now Staples Hill), again with six houses, and named after a family who once resided there. Pipehouse or Pipards had twelve houses and 'was likewise denominated from a family who anciently possessed it.' (Collinson).

Before the building of the Warminster Road (the A36) in the 1800s, a road ran from Trowbridge through Freshford to Bath. When it became a turnpike the level of the road was raised leaving the ground floor of some of the houses including the present post office below ground level. The road wound through Limpley Stoke and at the top of Crowe Hill there was a toll house – not though, as one would suspect, the house on the corner known as Honey Cottage which has all the imagined characterics of a building of this sort. Some time ago, long before its extension was built, this little octagonal house was covered with a thick thatch.

The road through the valley crosses the Frome near The Inn, the part of Freshford most familiar to visitors. This delightful combination of packhorse bridge, inn, farmland, water and history, sadly lost one of its treasured possessions about fifteen years ago when the centuries-old elm tree opposite the Inn succumbed to Dutch Elm Disease. It is hard to imagine that the small oak tree which now grows there will ever quite replace it.

The bridge and The Inn at Freshford.

Since its construction Freshford Bridge has withstood much traffic and many a flood. It replaced the first ford (from which Freshford may have got its name) on the Frome and was built sometime in the 1500s with money raised by the Prior of Hinton Charterhouse. It is said that he and the Abbot of Bath joined forces to raise funds, touring the countryside disguised as ordinary monks asking for alms.

Half a mile upstream from the bridge are two of the many mills on the Frome. For almost a thousand years Freshford Mill has been a place of employment. During the last fifty years it has been the Peradin Factory. The firm was evacuated here during the war and stayed on as a thriving polymer and rubber industry. Now, towards the end of the twentieth century, all work on the site of the ancient mill its likely to cease as the firm has now moved to other premises.

Nearby, on a side stream, is Dunkirk Mill, its name possibly derived from a building known as 'Dung Cart', with some unpleasant connotations. The mill has emerged from its cloak of ivy and has been lovingly and expertly restored to become individual flats. It now has three stories. The original five-storied building was depicted on a token issued in 1795 when a local magnate, Thomas Joyce who, in partnership with John Moggridge, was given permission to erect a mill to manufacture cloth. The token shows a picture of the mill on one side and the initials M. and J. and a fleece on the other.

Freshford has continued to thrive on and owes much of its existence to the cloth trade which was such a major influence in the life of the villages around the valley. Some of the great names in the industry, such as Methuen and Ashe, were closely associated with the village and for centuries most villagers were connected with the trade one way or another. Money from the wool industry provided additions to the church and many of the buildings which climb the hillsides.

The Old Parsonage on Church Hill, which used to be known as Gower (or Gowan) House, was built around 1630. One of the finest buildings from the eighteenth century is Ivythorpe opposite the church, its architecture is in the style of Bath buildings in the early Georgian period. The doorway has Tuscan pilasters which continue with Ionic pilasters above, as well as two other orders of pilasters. On the south-east corner by the church an attractive house with Gothick pointed windows stands opposite Morris' shop (now closed). Next to the church is Manor House, hidden at the end of its drive. Once the entrance was barred by splendid wrought iron gates dated 1903 but these were probably removed during the last war for ammunitions. What a loss!

The property known as Old House once encompassed many acres of the village. It has a plain Georgian front with pilasters at the angles of its nine windows. In the garden was a delightful gazebo which was very sadly demolished about twenty years ago.

The early 1800s saw the levying of a malt tax which effectively put paid to home brewing. Despite this, because of so much drunkeness in the 1870s the Temperance Society started the Village Room (above the Surgery) which offered Tea and Games Rooms. Between 1820-30, the Forster family built the brewery at the bottom of Church Hill, a building which to some extent still dominates the village with its tall chimney. It was shut down in the 1890s when it became both a factory for the manufacture of fertilisers and a rifle range. It is now a private residence.

View across Freshford from the church.

For many years, The Old Brewery has been the home of entrepreneur Jeremy Fry who renovated it some ten years ago, creating an exotic home including a seventy-foot long drawing room with a floor made of squares of leather. The house, which has workshops and offices on the lower floors, is a strange mixture of old and new, incorporating oriental and western objects. Mr. Fry was instrumental in rescuing Bath's Theatre Royal from near closure. He and his brother are descendants of the well-known chocolate family and were co-founders of the successful Rotork Engineering Company which pioneered and developed the famous squirrel wheelchair in conjunction with Lord Snowdon. Princess Margaret was an occasional visitor to The Old Brewery and a helicopter from the Queen's Flight could sometimes be seen hovering over the village. Now the building is being sold as Mr. Fry is moving to south-west India to grow cardamom and coffee and to build a replica of an old plantation home.

In 1849 an architect was sought to design and build Freshford School. Mr. Niblet, an architect more used to building churches, was found and incorporated various eccesiastical features into this fine school building. When it opened, eighty children between the ages of two and fourteen attended, with one teacher.

Freshford Station opened in 1857 and a double track was laid in the 1880s. From across the valley the station resembles something out of Toytown and although the railway is increasingly active with sprinter trains and rolling stock carrying aggregrate from the huge Somerset quarry near Frome, the busy lines and sidings of its heyday are past.

The Victorians and Edwardians of Bath considered Freshford, as well as other valley villages such as Bathford, to be a place of good, clean, rural living, particularly with regard to the purity of the air. For many decades the women of Freshford took in washing from town dwellers who felt a blow in the country air would be good for their linen. Landscape photos of that time include distant shots of lines of washing blowing in the wind.

Mixed farming around Freshford has given way to mainly grazing and cut grass. In June the valley hums with machines cutting neat swathes through the lush grass, leaving borders of pink campion, buttercup and wild parsley around the fields. The hedges are awash with musk rose and the numerous hidden paths around and through the village, its woods and fields, are well used.

Claverton

Lying between Monkton Combe and Bathampton, the Parish of Claverton, at present in the County of Avon, encompasses a large, roughly square, portion of the north facing slopes of the Limpley Stoke Valley and the Down above. Included within its boundaries are Bath University, The Bath Clinic, Claverton Pumping Station, The American Museum, the remains of Rainbow Wood belonging to the National Trust and the ancient village of Claverton. Below the thickly wooded upper slopes the magnificent parkland of the Manor extends down to the village and abuts the grasslands of the deer park to the west. There were deer here in the twelfth century when Claverton became the property of the Bishopric of Bath and was one of the manors allocated to the Bishop for his personal income and where he established a deer park.

St. Mary's Church shares its Rector with the church at Bathampton. The Parish Council, Parochial Church Council and Women's Institute serve the organisational needs of the Parish and twice a year there is a community get-together. Fund-raising activities include coffee mornings and Gardens Open to the Public. Yet this is a village that seems to have lost its heart. There is no shop, no post office, no school and the substantial community hall, built with such pride in 1958, is situated a mile from the village on the Down. The village population is largely comprised of commuters in new and converted properties, second home owners

117

and a few retired people. There are hardly any children and no facilities for them. It was not always so.

Below the village the A36 has been widened and a new wall and fence erected to lessen the sound of traffic that has increased in volume and speed. Hidden behind this barrier, Claverton almost disappeared from view; but behind the wall, and through the large imposing gate posts topped with finials and known as Ralph Allen's pillars, there lurks a fascinating history.

With no reasonable evidence of Roman occupation, the village is thought to date from Saxon times. It is estimated from the Domesday Survey that in 1086 there were about a hundred inhabitants. In 1791, according to Collinson's *History of Somerset*, the population was still a hundred and there were sixteen houses.

Essentially the history of Claverton is one of an agricultural community in a well-sheltered valley with fertile land near the river, the river well-stocked with fish, an abundant water-supply, timber and clay for building and an island in the river navigable by early standards, which provided easy means of making fords and bridges, increased facilties for fishing, and allowed the erection of a dam for the mill without impeding navigation.   (*The History of Claverton*)

Claverton Pumping Station.

Estate accounts, which have survived from the fourteenth century, include mention of the sale of woodland, crops and hay. The 'Hay Feast' used to be held annually, particularly at the end of the nineteenth century, but there is no record as to when this highly appropriate festival started in a village where hay-cropping has had such importance.

In 1608 the manor, which in 1548 had passed from the Bishopric to the Crown, was acquired by William Bassett. So began the long association of the Bassett family with Claverton, (a name familiar to travellers on the A36 as they pass Bassett House which was once a hotel). William, his son and grandson all resided on the estate and it is to them that Claverton owed the beautiful Manor House which, tragically, was demolished in 1819, and also the famous vineyard which gave its name to Vineyard Farm and Vineyard Bottom. The vineyard, including the layout of the planted vines, is nicely illustrated in Thorpe's Map of Bath drawn in 1742.

When William Bassett II died in 1656 the estate was in grave financial difficulty and, on the death of his son William Bassett III in 1693, the estate was sold to Richard Holder of Bathampton to pay the debts. The name of Skrine first enters the history of Claverton when Dr. Skrine acquired the manor in 1714, a name that is familiar on both sides of the river, particularly in connection with Warleigh Manor.

Dr. Skrine, a wealthy physician, and known as the 'great apothecary of Bath', died in 1735 leaving Claverton to his son who sold it to Ralph Allen in 1758. Allen's connection with Claverton produced 'The Avenue' – a road he built between Prior Park, where he continued to live, and Claverton which he visited once a week. He was generous to the parish, particularly the church, which he presented with a stone altar, font, reredos and gallery. Many eminent people from Bath chose to be buried in the little churchyard overlooking the valley at Claverton, and there were grumbles in the village that in some years non-resident burials easily outnumbered those from the parish. Ralph Allen was no exception and his large mausoleum, admittedly shared with others, takes up a large amount of space.

Ralph Allen built a school in Claverton for his friend the Rev. Richard Graves who was the incumbent of Claverton from 1749 until his death in 1805. The school, run by this man of outstanding ability, was a great success – so much so that he had to rent the Manor House where forty little boys had their dormitory. Among others, his most famous pupil was Thomas Malthus, the well known writer on population theories.

With his attractive personality and prolific literary ability, it was surprising that Richard Graves remained in the small village of Claverton as its Rector for over fifty years. He wrote light verse and novels, earning a place in the *Cambridge History of English Literature* with his best seller *The Spiritual Quixote*. Much of his writing was done in the garden of the Old Rectory where he built a summerhouse called The Chantry. He was, by his own admission, a poor preacher, but was a kind and compassionate Rector. During his long incumbency, he took an active part in looking after the poor of the parish. He administered the poor relief efficiently and generously and Claverton had a reputation for never sending its poor to the workhouse but cared for them within their own community.

In the eighteenth century Ralph Allen's famous quarries on Claverton Down became a tourist attraction, as did the two-mile race track which, among others, was frequented by the population of Bath. The Down was also the haunt of high-waymen and pickpockets. The race-course is distinctly marked on Thorpe's 1742 Map of Bath showing the rectangular two-mile track with another track across its centre to produce a one-mile course. There was a grandstand, stables and other amusements such as a fair-ground and refreshments. In 1784 it was abandoned in favour of the more convenient site on Lansdown. Cricket was also played on the Down including matches, such as Somerset Against All England, played in 1774. As for the highwaymen, the most famous of them was John Poulter, who would wait at the top of Brassknocker Hill and rob coaches and carriages as they made the sharp turn to descend the hill. He was caught and hanged and his body hung in chains at the end of Lime Kiln Lane.

Today, among the renovated barns of the old farming community and some lovely eighteenth century architecture, the old village of Claverton can be detected. The wrought-iron gates and thirty steps of the old Manor House are firm reminders of the past. There is a water-colour drawing of the old Manor House in the British Museum. It was built from the design of John of Padua, who also built Kingstone House in Bradford-on-Avon. It was flanked by the medieval church on one side and by its massive tythe barn on the other. Through its splendid gateway, which still exists, there are thirty old stone steps which rose to the front door. The house existed into the early nineteenth century when it was bought by John Vivian. He intended to restore the old Manor House but was persuaded by his architect, Sir Jeffry Wyattville, to demolish it and build a new one at a higher level. The famous Rector of Camerton, the Rev. John Skinner, was curate of Claverton at that time and he objected strongly to this destruction. So did Vivian's son George, who managed to retain the steps and gates, the pillars of which are similar to those on the main road. It is a tradition that the ornaments on top denote hospitality and are an invitation to beggars to a free meal, a common practice in the seventeenth century.

Looking through the gates a Victorian church stands where once there was a Norman then medieval church. There is clear view of the field where the Manor stood and its old farm buildings, including its now unrecognisable tythe barn, are private dwellings. Where the park-land reaches down to the village street there is a gate with a sign saying Old Rectory Garden – Private. Sadly, the large, once exquisite garden, enclosed by mellowing brick walls, is now derelict and overgrown. Roses still cascade over mounds which were terraced walls of stone and the round pond is, surprisingly, still full of water. But Richard Graves' summer house has gone and this neglected place is being absorbed by nature.

The new Manor House has a well-deserved place in the history of Claverton. On January 21st, 1956, the death of Miss Skrine, the last surviving member of the family who became squires of Claverton in 1873 and lived in the new house, caused widespead grief. The estate, which had remained intact since Saxon times, was broken up and the Manor House was sold. This event served to hasten the demise of a once thriving agricultural community which was perhaps already in decline. So often an indicator of the decline of a village is the fate of its school. In 1898 a new school was opened with forty pupils. At one time this rose to fifty-two but in 1950, perhaps due to improved transport to Bath, there were only six and it closed soon after. The population on the Down continued to grow and in 1951 part of this area was included in the City of Bath. The Parish Church in the village was too far for most people and a pre-fabricated church (now demolished) was built on the Down.

The view from Claverton's old Manor House.

In 1957 Claverton Manor was bought by Dr. Dallas Pratt who had a deep appreciation of the American arts and a desire to increase Anglo-American understanding. In 1961 he opened the Museum of American Arts and Crafts, now known as the American Museum in Britain. It is supported by Friends in both countries and, in co-operation with schools and colleges, has an active educational programme. Despite the decline of the village, the success of the new Manor House, with its thousands of annual visitors, has brought Claverton international fame. This house, where Sir Winston Churchill made his first political speech, stands high above the village with magnificent views of the valley. It is surrounded by woods, gardens and a vast lawn which spreads down to the parkland below. On a misty day, the drive from its entrance gates to the house is strangely reminiscent of the famous American Blue Ridge Parkway, lined as it is with rhododendrons, with a deep drop to the valley below and a distant view of the wooded ridge to the north.

Re-enactment of battle from the American Civil War on Claverton Down, 1993.

Monkton Combe

In a narrow valley in the hills, half a mile from where the Midford Brook flows quietly into the River Avon, the village of Monkton Combe spreads itself along the valley floor and dots the neighbouring hillside. It is apart from, yet part of, the magnificent Avon Valley landscape. Until 1974 it was in Somerset but, for the time being, has been placed in the County of Avon.

Despite its distant associations with Roman Bath and its continuation as a settlement from that time, great historical events have passed it by. Even its long connection with the monastery and the monks of Bath throughout medieval times produced little more than some interesting monastic farm buildings. It was not a feudal village and had no great house or family and it was not until the middle of the nineteenth century that Monkton Combe began to lose its anonymity. The Rev. Francis Pocock, a remarkable clergyman and incumbent at that time, entirely rebuilt the church, built a vicarage for himself and founded a school for boys. From that time, the name of Monkton Combe became well known to generations of school boys and their families.

In 1791 the Rev. John Collinson, in his *History of Antiquities in the County of Somerset*, wrote about the village:

This place is generally called Monkton-Combe, the adjunct being placed first; but its simple proper name is Combe, the other having been added to signify its belonging to the monks of Bath, and to distinguish it from other places of similar appellation.

He described its delightful situation, its close proximity to the stone quarries on Combe Down and the view from

an elegant mansion called Combe-Grove, belonging to Mrs. Simpson of Bath.... The prospect from this spot, over the vale and the slope of the opposite range of hills, is very beautiful. On the summit of Combe-down, a mile northward from the church, among many immense quarries of fine free stone, are large groves of firs, planted by the late Ralph Allen, esq. for the laudable purpose of ornamenting this (at that time rough and barren) hill. Among these groves is a neat range of buildings belonging to this parish. It consists of eleven houses, built of wrought stone, raised on the spot; each of which has a small garden in front. These were originally built for the workmen employed in the quarries, but are now chiefly let to invalids from Bath, who retire hither for the sake of a very fine air from which many have received essential benefit. The surrounding beautiful and extensive prospects, the wild, but pleasing irregularities of the surface and scenery, diversified with immense quarries, fine open cultivated fields, and extensive plantations of firs, which throw a solemn gloominess of shade impervious to the sun and winds, over a fine soft turf free from underwood, all serve to render this a delightful summer retreat.

The view today from the gardens of Bathite Cottages is breathtaking. It is hard though to find the 'best' view of Monkton Combe. By descending Brassknocker Hill, the Limpley Stoke Valley is seen to stretch away towards Bradford on Avon with the village nestling in the Midford Valley below. Alternatively, ascending the road above the village to Combe Down and pausing at the old Tythe Barn, where the 'drung' descends steeply to the village, is perhaps the most pleasing view. There again, go along Waterhouse Lane and, with the splendid arches of the viaduct on the right, the village is seen across the brook against the backdrop of hills and woods which rise 500 feet above it.

In 1924 two clergymen, the Rev. D. Lee Pitcairn and the Rev. Alfred Richardson produced *A Historical Guide to Monkton Combe, Combe Down and Claverton*. This was a well researched history of a little known village. As it had for Collinson in 1791, the Domesday Book of 1086 provided valuable information:

The Church itself hold Cume. In the time of King Edward it paid geld (i.e. tax) for 9 hides of land. There is land for 8 ploughs. Of it there are in demesne 6 hides. And there are 3 ploughs and 6 serfs and 7 villeins and 8 boors with five ploughs. There are two mills paying 13 shilling and 6 pence and 32 acres of meadow and 1 mile of small wood in length and breadth. It is worth 6 pounds of rent now 8 pounds.

The authors of the Guide also defined the name of the village:

In the Domesday Book Monkton Combe is referred to as CUME meaning 'valley'. Monkton, prefixed to the old name, was to distinguish it from other similarly named places, and particularly because the place was from ancient times monastic property. In the old register belonging to the Church, commencing 1561, the name is written 'Moncken Combe' i.e. Monk's Combe, using the old form of the plural of 'monk' like 'oxen' from 'ox'. This may have been altered to Monkton in order to bring it into line with the many names of places which end in TON. In whatever way the name is spelt, however, it preserves the history of the place, that nine centuries ago and for long afterwards it belonged to the monks of Bath.

The Normans built a small church here but there was no monastery and it is likely that the manor was used as a demesne farm tended by the monks of Bath. For five centuries they tended their sheep, grew vegetables and ground corn in the mills, carrying the produce up the hill footpath known as 'the drung' (still in use today) to the grange on the hill above. Here they would store the produce before removing it to the Priory in Bath. The other group of monastic buildings were in the valley below. Close to the church stands the monks' farmhouse, now known as Monks' Retreat, the older portion of which predates 1490. In the farmyard to the west is a group of ancient farm buildings including a barn and a dovecot or pigeon house. The 'drung' between the two groups

Monk's Retreat, Monkton Combe.

of buildings is a fragment of the old public road between Bath and Warminster. The continuation of it can be detected crossing the meadow to what used to be a packhorse bridge over the brook. This was replaced by a wooden bridge after the first was swept away in floods a few years ago. The path continues straight up the other side of the valley slope with banks and hedges on either side.

It is hard to ignore the influence that the church has had on the history of the village. It would seem that Monkton Combe would not exist in its present form and certainly would not have been so well documented, without the help of interested churchmen. Its desmene farm belonging to the church in Bath; its chroniclers – the Revs. Collinson, Pitcairn and Richardson; its philanthopist the Rev. Pocock and, last but not least, the Rev. Percy Warrington, vicar of Monkton Combe for forty-three years between 1918 and 1961, have all contributed greatly to the life of the village.

On November 19, 1961 an article appeared in the *Observer* newspaper:

> The other day the Rev. Percy Warrington, Vicar of Monkton Combe in Somerset, died in a nursing home in Bath at the age of seventy-two. A short man with a bald patch surrounded by long straggly hair, which made him look rather like a Cruikshank caricature of a curate, Warrington had been the incumbent of this small country parish for forty-three years. The announcement of his death caused scarcely a ripple of interest.
>
> Yet this was the greatest school-founder of the century. During the twenties, in his early years at Monkton Combe, he founded public schools at the rate of one a year. Stowe, Canford, Westonbirt, Wrekin, Felixstowe, Harrogate: he launched or bought them all – and more besides...... But for Percy Warrington these schools would not exist today. Yet none of them was represented at his funeral.

At the age of thirty-one the Rev. Warrington had announced that he wanted to found schools, a university college and a theological college as well as old people's homes. Before he was forty-five he had done all these things. (It should be noted, above, that Monkton Combe School was not founded by the Rev. Warrington.)

Warrington was not stretched in his duties as vicar of Monkton Combe and this allowed time to turn his talents and great organisational abilities to his various projects. He was an unbending rigid Protestant who wanted to win people to his church through education. He had no money but had a magnetism that carried people with him and he became known as 'the financier in a surplice'. His many faceted character often drew less than complimentary comments from those who knew him. Descriptions varied from 'pompous', 'mentally unhinged' (this from his solicitor), to 'talented' and 'gifted'. He was also resourceful and managed to raise money by way of mortgage and guarantee on the properties of one school to advance to another school. In this way he raised hundreds of thousands of pounds.

His fellow trustees became concerned at the speed in which he pushed ahead with his plans and the power he had secured for himself. The Legal and General Assurance Company stood guarantor for £1 million and they also became worried. When he eventually overstretched himself and used the schools' money for other purposes the trustees vowed to get rid of him. For the sake of the schools, the parents were told nothing but from that time the name of Percy Warrington was expunged from the records.

He remained in Monkton Combe for the rest of his life and, although difficult to get on with, won the respect of many, particularly the poorer people whom he championed. He did not neglect his church or his parishioners and he was the main force behind the building of the substantial village hall. He also ran the village cricket team. His eccentric behaviour came through occasionally with such projects as the installation, at his home at Westfield House, of an entire water-garden from Chelsea Flower Show. He lived in style and drove around in a yellow Daimler known to locals as the Yellow Peril.

Cricket on Monkton Combe School playing field near the Viaduct.

In his early years in Monkton Combe Warrington had lived in splendour in a mansion called Waterhouse on the south side of the valley. He never married but shared the house with two maiden ladies. After a tussle with the Bishop of Bath and Wells he was required to leave this house, which was in the parish of Freshford, and live within his own parish. His ambition to set up old people's homes eventually came to fruition in his later years when Waterhouse became a residential home for the elderly, along with another in Corsham. These homes can still be found in the telephone book under the name of Percy Warrington Trust. He died at Waterhouse at the age of seventy-two. Although none of the great schools he founded were represented at his funeral, fittingly, representatives from the homes in which he took such a pride were there to pay their last respects to this gifted and extraordinary man.

Limpley Stoke

The village of Limpley Stoke, from which the valley takes it name, is situated close to the mid-point of the valley, some two miles from Bradford on Avon. It lies to the west of Winsley and here, on the bend of the river where the gorge is narrow, the land rises steeply to the west. Upper Stoke, Middle Stoke and Lower Stoke are joined by pathways, steps and steep little roads, giving the appearance of a mountain village, their houses partly hidden in the trees on the wooded slopes. Above Middle Stoke is the main road from Bath to Warminster and below it, the railway runs parallel with the river. Although in the shade of the hill for much of the winter, the village enjoys spectacular views of the river and valley especially when bathed in sunlight.

The parish of Limpley Stoke shares with Freshford a triangular piece of Wiltshire that intrudes into the County of Avon. Within its boundaries are the River Avon, a section of the canal, Midford Lane as far as Midford, and the Midford Valley west of the Brook. The immense Selwood Forest which bordered the parish in the past, is apparent in the clusters of woodland left untouched such as Slit-terns Wood, Donleaze Wood and the woods around Cleeve Rocks close to Midford Lane. These important woodlands have been designated Sites of Special Scientific Interest because they contain some of the best examples of southern calcareous ash wych elm found on the oolitic limestone. The entire parish is covered by the Green Belt Policy and is in both an Area of Outstanding Natural Beauty and of High Ecological Value.

The name Limpley Stoke has puzzled place-name experts. The name used in Saxon times was *stoc* or *stock*. The original meaning of this is 'place' but is also found in the sense of 'monastery' or 'cell' and could therefore be of ecclesiastic origin. Richard Hooker, in his *History of Limpley Stoke*, suggests the meaning 'a stockaded place near a wood'. 'Stoke' is derived from *Stock*, and *Wina's Ley Stoke* and *Hanging Stock* are both found in Domesday. The first suggests a connection with Winsley, and the *ley* or *leah* being a 'clearing or open space'. Various maps and records, including one in 1322, contain the names Hanging Stoke, Winsley Stoke and Stoke. It is not until 1585 that the name Limply or Limpley Stoke appears. In 1578 Elizabeth I :

> granted to John Mersche and John Turpyn a ruined chapel called 'Our Lady of Limpley's Chapel' and a small house once called the church house of Hanging Stock, or Stoke-upon-Avon, which had recently been occupied by persons responsible for maintaining the offering and lights before the image of our Lady of Limpley Stoke. (VHCW)

The house, which was close to the church on its east side, at the top of the field known as Limpley Field, is shown on the tythe map of 1841 and listed as 'Old house, and garden', belonging to Robert Cooper and Joseph Clisild Daniel.

By the end of the century it had been demolished. There is no knowing when the house was built or whether the Limpley family lived in it.

Limpley Stoke's history dates from Roman times and the Roman road between Bath and Poole passed close to Cleeve Rocks where, in a field known as Money Groves, there are remains of a Roman settlement. Roman tiles and other finds in Limpley Field suggest another settlement near the church. The Saxons, who built their little church on the hill, were overtaken by the Normans who added a doorway to the building. Like so many others, their numbers were no doubt decimated by the Black Death and the settlement only sprang back to life with the coming of the weaving industry around 1400 A.D. From that time the village gradually extended downhill towards the river. By 1614 a fulling mill had been established and Stoke was a thriving community of weavers.

Limpley Stoke and Winsley were originally included in the ancient parish of Bradford and paid tythes accordingly to the Abbess of Shaftesbury. In 1894 the urban area of Bradford was constituted a separate parish and named Bradford Without. The same year the area was divided into five new parishes, that of Holt, South Wraxall, Winsley, Limpley Stoke and Bradford Without. In 1934, Limpley Stoke and Winsley, with other neighbouring Wiltshire parishes, became part of the parish of Melksham which included Bradford and was known as Bradford and Melksham Rural District. The parishes are now administered by the West Wiltshire District Council.

In 1977 schoolboy Richard Hooker completed a local history project on *Limpley Stoke from Roman Times to the Present Day* and circulated fifty copies around the village. Many people would like to see this manuscript published as this is the most definitive work of any of the villages in the valley. The whole parish is covered – including the quarries, lost buildings, old field names, the Hydro, the railway and the canal, and the history of almost every building is described in detail. The part of the village known as Middle Stoke is the narrow picturesque street which runs between the church and the Warminster Road near The Rose and Crown. The settlement extended naturally downhill from the church and it is here the oldest weavers' cottages are found, some dating back to 1550. During the 1840s, much renovation of these ranks of cottages, such as Forster's Buildings, was undertaken by the principal landowners of the time – Robert Cooper and John Fisher.

The school, the old village shop, The Rose and Crown Inn, the Baptist Chapel, the Bakery, The Village Hall, and of course the village well – all were, or are still found in Middle Stoke. The 'springline settlement' was blessed with numerous surface streams issuing from the vast underground network of fresh water springs on the hillside. The village well at Middle Stoke served the needs of the community, not only as a constant source of fresh water but as a favourite meeting place. For centuries this well and others in the village were the only source of water until 1935 when the village went on the main supply.

Lower Stoke covers the largest part of the village and runs from Crowe Hill to Winsley Bridge and includes the mill, railway station, manor estate, the Post Office Stores, the Hop Pole Inn and The Limpley Stoke Hotel. Richard Hooker speculates on the possibility of a monastery or some other large medieval building or buildings having once been situated somewhere between the Hop Pole Inn and Lower Hayze. Evidence for this is the remains of what could have been a med-ieval fish pool associated with a monastery. Also, the Manor and many of the oldest cottages in this part of the village have large cellars with thick walls dating from an earlier time. Alternatively, he wonders if the buildings could be of Roman origin associated with a Roman ford.

It is interesting to note the division of property in the nineteenth century. In 1840 the Lord of the Manor, Sir John Cam Hobhouse, had his seat in Bradford on Avon and owned at least 483 acres of land in the Borough Tithing and the outer hamlets. Each of the hamlets also had its 'mansion' or Manor House, owned and usually lived in by a 'principal landowner' – a family that was looked upon as 'gentry'. Most landowners owned a great deal of property and some were considered more highly that others in the social order. As Gee Langdon makes clear in her *Year of the Map*, there was a subtle distinction between gentry and the mere yeoman farmer. High in the social ranking in Limpley Stoke in the 1840s were John Penruddock, Robert Cooper, Joseph Clisild Daniel and Henry Too-good Davis. These people were usually accorded 'Esquire' after their name, as seen in the Listing of Landowners and Occupiers on Ashmead's Tythe Map of 1841. Henry and John Fisher, also wealthy landowners, did not have 'Esquire' after their name.

The Tithing for Limpley Stoke listed 190 properties which included all arable land, pasture, orchards, woodland, wasteland and buildings. Out of these, Robert Cooper, Esq., owned ninety-one, including the Manor House. Forty-two of these properties he owned jointly with Henry and John Fisher, twenty-one with Joseph Clisild Daniel, Esq. (a joint owner of the Manor), and the rest he either shared with various other people or was the sole owner. Joseph Clisild Daniel, a local inventor, who for a while owned the Mill at Limpley Stoke, also owned much of Conkwell Woods and other property on that hillside. Henry Toogood Davis, Esq. is listed as having thirty-one properties, most of them entirely his own.

John Penruddock Esq. is listed as having a part or whole share in only five properties. He lived at Lower Hayze (joint ownership with Robert Cooper) where it is said he entertained his close friend Lord Nelson and Nelson's even closer friend, Lady Hamilton. Not only was John Penruddock considered to be 'gentry', he was also the 'most looked up to' person in the neighbourhood.

One key part of Limpley Stoke owned by Robert Cooper and Henry and John Fisher, was 'Stoke Farm house, and homestead'. The farm was between Middle and Lower Stoke when most of that part of Limpley Stoke was woodland, known as Pucklewood, and much of it, including orchards and pasture, was in joint

Above: The West of England Hydropathic Establishment, 1892;
Below: A tennis party posing for the camera, 1892;
Opposite: pages from the Hydro brochure.

West of England Hydropathic Establishment,

Limpley Stoke, near Bath.

LIMPLEY STOKE is situate in the most picturesque part of Wiltshire, on a tongue or neck of that County running into Somersetshire; Limpley Stoke Station is 6 miles from Bath, on the Bath and Salisbury Branch of the Great Western Railway.

The Hydropathic Establishment is only three minutes' walk from the Station, and the Post and Telegraph Office is close to the entrance gates.

This Health Resort was founded in the year 1860, the locality being specially selected as affording the essential requisites of convenience of access, abundance of pure water, and a climate equable in temperature and mild in winter.

The Grounds are 14 acres in extent, and command most beautiful views of the valley of the Avon, and the walks and drives in the immediate neighbourhood in all directions are very picturesque. Visitors invariably express surprise and pleasure at the beauty of the scenery.

As a Residence this Hydro. has great and important advantages over Hotels, Boarding-houses, and Lodgings, in its spacious grounds and facilities for tennis, boating, and other out-door amusements, and particularly in the number and size of its Public Rooms, which are of large proportions and include Drawing-Room, 40 x 22 feet; Dining Room, 37 x 20 feet; Reading Room, 26 x 20 feet; Recreation Room, 50 x 30 feet; Billiard Room (full-sized table), Ladies' Drawing Room, Cloak Rooms, Lavatories, &c.

Conversation being prohibited in the very commodious and comfortable Reading and Writing Room, guests disposed for quiet can insure it here, while those who are socially inclined will be glad to know that the great majority of visitors join in the friendly intercourse for which this Establishment is celebrated.

The Passages, &c., are warmed to 60° in winter.

THE BATHS

in separate departments for ladies and gentlemen, have been recently re-constructed on a large scale, and include Turkish, Russian, Needle, Spray, Lamp, Douche, Sulphur, Electric, and other Hydropathic Appliances. Massage and Rubbing are also administered by experienced Masseurs—male and female.

PATIENTS

suffering from Indigestion, Gout, Rheumatism, want of sleep, debility, depression of spirits, or otherwise out of health, should seek restoration at this Hydropathic Home, under the constant care of a Resident Physician, a Manageress of large experience, and in the company of the strong, the healthy, and the cheerful.

Although medicines are administered in cases where they are deemed essential, the constant endeavour is to promote health by the simplest and most natural methods.

VISITORS

desiring only change and a pleasant resting place, will also find here what they require, the comforts of home away from home. An abundant table served with strict punctuality Out-door amusements, beautiful scenery and cheerful society, with close proximity to Bath, Bristol, and Clifton, for occasional resort to city life.

DOMESTIC ARRANGEMENTS.

BREAKFAST, 8.30, in Winter, 9; LUNCH, 1.30; AFTERNOON TEA, 4; DINNER, 6.30.

Sundays:—DINNER, 1.15; TEA 5.30; SUPPER, 8.30.

FAMILY WORSHIP at 9.15 A.M. and 8.45 P.M.

The Drill Instructor attends from 10 to 10.30 a.m , to drill and exercise in Calisthenics with piano accompaniment, free of charge.

The extensive Grounds afford ample space for promenade.

Carriages and Saddle Horses may be had at unusually moderate charges.

Pleasant excursions may be made to Hinton Abbey, Farleigh Castle, Bradford-on-Avon with its Saxon and Flemish antiquities, Wells and its Cathedral, Cheddar and its far-famed rocks and caves, Longleat, Salisbury Cathedral, Stonehenge, Clifton, Bath, &c.

Persons suffering or recovering from Infectious Diseases, or Unsound Mind, or otherwise unsuitable, are not admitted.

Dogs are not allowed in the House.

Further Particulars on application. Letters should be addressed "The Manager," and Telegrams, "Hydro., Limpley-Stoke, Bath."

A Porter attends all Trains.

Cooper/Fisher ownership. Somewhere in the area of the farmhouse there had been a 'spa' where people went for treatment for rheumatic pain. Although the Tythe Map shows numerous outbuildings near the farm, they are not listed as being part of a treatment centre.

In the1860s a lavish Victorian Hydro was built consisting of a series of buildings and treatment rooms and a large house in the middle (part of which was the Stoke Farmhouse), surrounded by grounds covering seven acres of hillside. The water from the streams was gathered in large tanks on the hill above to supply water for the Turkish Baths and the main buildings. Streams and waterfalls, terraces and tennis courts, gravelled paths and flower beds and even clock golf courses were created for the flock of visitors who came to stay at The West of England Hydropathic Establishment. A brochure with photographs was produced and it is fascinating to see the facilities and treatments on offer.

The mania for Hydros lasted well into this century but during the 1920s it was becoming a thing of the past. In 1936 the Hydro closed down and much of the land sold, including the Withy Batch which was eventually bought by the Parish Council as land for a Children's Playing Field. This purchase had been in celebration of the late King George V and it was opened on George VI's Coronation Day in 1937. It must be the steepest children's playing field in England and almost certainly has the best view.

Upper Stoke is the part of the parish above and to the west of the Warminster Road where the woods cling to the precipate cliff face. On the flat land at the top of the ridge is a cluster of attractive, post-war houses and bungalows. In this area, where the Midford Lane joins the Warminster Road at the top of the hill, are the remains of the old quarries. In the eighteenth and nineteenth centuries, Stoke Hill Quarry and Hayes Wood Quarry, both of which were in Freshford parish, produced a vast network of underground tunnels covering many acres of land around Midford Lane. These were deep underground quarries which extracted coarse limestone. There were three open quarries in Limpley Stoke parish, one of which was further down the lane past Cleeve Rocks. The other two were on the hillside at Middle Stoke.

This part of the parish extends south past Cleeve Rocks as far as Midford. From here it is possible to walk back along the parish boundary, down the fertile valley of the Midford Brook to the Avon Valley. The footpath passes the remains of the Camerton and Limpley Stoke Railway, skirts the edge of Slitterns Wood and the fields of Brett Farm with its lovely old Tythe Barn, before continuing down towards Waterhouse.

In 1614 Limpley Stoke Mill was sold to Richard Dicke, a wealthy Turleigh clothier, and was still owned by the Dicke family (now called Dyke) in 1784 when it was sold to Henry Fisher. In 1796 it passed to John Newton who rebuilt it as a factory. He was a partner in the firm Bush, Newton and Bush whose thriving business allowed them to employ at least two hundred by the year 1816. After mixed fortunes the mill was sold in 1835 to the Bradford firm of Saunders, Tanner and Co. who were made bankrupt during the hard times of the 1840s. Joseph Clisild Daniel (see above) and his son bought the mill and experimented, unsuccessfully, with the first water-powered loom. By then the woollen trade had almost ceased in the area and for about twenty-five years the mill for almost derelict. It was then owned by the Edmonds family who sold it in 1875 to Giles Holbrow, a timber merchant. Besides using part of the building as a saw mill, he also began to manufacture rubber and within five years the India Rubber Co. was launched.

The expanding business soon moved to Melksham although the saw mill continued to be worked. In 1895 the Rubber Mill was once again in business – the chimney stack was built and the new firm was named The Avon Rubber Company. In 1938 the timber mill was gutted by fire and soon afterwards the rubber mill became derelict. The old, tall chimney stack, which appears in many, relatively recent photographs and drawings, was demolished in 1961. After another spell as a timber and fencing works and further decay, the mill has been completely and sympathetically renovated and is now used as offices for the software consultancy Microtec.

Limpley Stoke Mill, sympathetically restored in recent years.

Winsley

The familiar cover of the Winsley Parish magazine, *The Winsley Weaver*, shows a signpost with four arms below the name of Winsley. They point to Turleigh, Murhill, Conkwell, and Ashley and Haugh. This large Wiltshire parish incorporates these five hamlets as it stretches for two miles along the uneven escarpment on the north side of the valley with the village of Winsley situated some two miles from Bradford on Avon.

Winsley is separated from the more south-easterly settlement of Turleigh by a steep, wooded slope. Murhill lies south of Winsley, its houses clinging to the hillside overlooking the Limpley Stoke Valley. The outlying hamlet of Conkwell lies due north in a cleft in the valley's rim, its single street being the border where Wiltshire meets Avon and the division between Warleigh and Conkwell Woods.

Winsley and its surrounding area is of great scientific and ecological interest. The flat agricultural land to the north is designated a Special Landscape Area. To the west of the village is an Area of High Ecological Value. Close to the old Winsley Hospital (now Avon Park), the woods that hide the Murhill stone quarry and its workings are designated a Site of Special Scientific Interest. So too is the semi-natural woodland at Warleigh Woods where, amongst the trees and buried in thick undergrowth near Inwoods are the prehistoric remains of Neolithic and Roman sites. The parish lies in an Area of Oustanding Natural Beauty and is covered by the Green Belt.

The manor of Winsley or Winsley-cum-Turleigh formed part of the manor of Bradford during the Middle Ages. After the Dissolution, the grant of Bradford to Sir Edward Bellingham in 1546 included appurtenances in Winsley. By 1758 an unknown part of the the manor was conveyed to Sir Robert Long and Walter Long. This may have been passed as part of the manor of South Wraxall of which Walter Long was lord. In 1828 a manor of Winsley was said to belong to John Hayes Dunkin and James Baber (VHCW). The Bradford Parish tythe map of 1841, which included the Winsley tything, stated that there were fifty-three farms. Ten of these farm holdings were in Winsley and most were run by tenant farmers. Much of the land was owned by a handful of wealthy landowners such as Ann Atwood (see below), James Baber, who owned Winsley Manor and much more besides, and the joint ownership of some farms by John Pinchin and James Antrobus.

On the flat plateau to the north of the village are the small, scattered groups of houses of Haugh and Ashley, both once sizeable villages. The name 'Haugh', pronounced 'hay', means hedge or enclosure and was probably derived from John de la Haghe who owned Haugh Farm in 1281. An old coach road leads past the farm and an ancient building close by was once a chapel, possibly of some note as many footpaths converge on it. The manor of Ashley originated as an estate held by the Abbey of Shaftesbury. Roger de Asselegh was a tenant at Bradford in 1280. He was possibly an ancestor of Hugh de Ashley who died in 1493 and who had held the manor of Ashley (VHCW). Over time these once thriving agricultural settlements have lost their village status and we are left with isolated farms and houses, some magnificent Cotswold stone farm buildings such as the barn at Little Ashley Farm, and a multiplicity of stone walls which bind the fertile fields and copses of the plateau.

The Conservation Area that incorporates the old village of Winsley is connected to Turleigh Conservation Area at its eastern boundary. It is interesting to note the purpose of designation of a Conservation Area which is 'to conserve and enhance the special architectural or historic qualities of the area'. In the case of Winsley account must be taken of another settlement consisting of three separate estates, built over the last fifty years, which has grown up alongside the old village, greatly increasing the overall population. There is surprising cohesion between the old and the new and a fairly happy compromise with the sharing of village amenities. The school and shops have moved from the old village to the new while the old retains the village hall, the bowls club, the cricket club, the social club and of course the Parish and Methodist churches.

The immediate and obvious difference in the two parts of the village is the architecture. The houses in the new part of the village are – well, new. Estates by definition have a sameness about them, although they can be pleasant places in which to live. Consider, in contrast, the uniqueness of each building in the

Winsley Flower Show in the village hall, 1992.

old village. The character of the old Cotswold stone buildings is also in their attractive grouping, particularly around the Seven Stars public house, the adjacent granary, the seventeenth century Manor House and the even older Manor Farm, the church and Church Cottages. The narrow lane which starts at the church and winds past old cottages, some with mansard roofs where the weavers worked, ends at a high wall behind which is the mellowing stone of a rambling Elizabethan house known as Burghope. Some of the old yew trees that were originally planted to mark a paved walk between Burghope and the Manor are still apparent, particularly the tree in the Seven Stars car park and in the gardens of Barn House and Scarth.

The romance of myth and legend is sometimes more appealing that plain historical fact and there is a story in Winsley that has been perpetuated over the years. The following comes from the *Winsley Scrapbook*:

Tradition tells of a great battle fought between the Saxons and the Danes at Turleigh Crossroads and the lane below still bears the name Dane's Bottom. In the field near this site – north east of Winsley Church – earthworks and trenches formerly existed, and swords and weapons are reported to have been found there. In the three-cornered plot of land known as 'The Piece', through which the footpath passes from Winsley to Turleigh, King Alfred is said to have signed a proclamation of 'Peace' with his foes. The field should therefore be called 'The Peace'.

Another story is connected with Winsley Manor, the lovely old Elizabethan house which was then owned by the Knatchbull family. Again, this item comes from the *Winsley Scrapbook*:

A clairvoyant once stayed as a guest at the Manor. By automatic writing she located a ring buried under the drive, and a ring of old fashioned design was found. The house was supposed to be haunted by a lady in a brown silk dress, who walked up the back stairs seeking something. After the ring was found she was at rest. The clairvoyant said that the ring must be buried with Mrs. Knatchbull or the lady would wander again. Mrs. Knatchbull died on April 25th 1958, and the ring was put on her finger and buried with her.

Providing a continuity with old village traditions is the thriving bowling green which is adjacent to the outdated but much used village hall. Despite its inadequate facilities the hall, like most village halls, provides space for such varied activities as playgroup, Cub and Scout meetings, badminton, WI, the annual Fruit, Vegetable and Flower show and Barn Dances. Plays, pantomimes, and recently, a high-standard production of 'The Mikado', have all been extremely popular.

Lanes and paths provide a variety of delightful walks in all directions, particularly south into the valley where footpaths link up with the canal towpath and riverside trackways. Winsley could and should be a haven of tranquility but for one serious problem – heavy traffic. It does not, yet, have a by-pass.

'Few subjects are more emotive and raise more wrath and division that that of a by-pass,' words spoken about sixteen years ago by Sir Hugo Marshall, long time resident of Murhill, as he addressed yet another public meeting about the long awaited by-pass. Suffice to say that after thirty years of discussion, argument, public inquiries, press and T.V. coverage and monumental files on the subject of Winsley's by-pass, only two-thirds of the road have been built. Through blunders, mistakes, 'technical errors' and the inevitable lack of money the village has a splendid section of by-pass which leads nowhere. No amount of cajoling, letter-writing, reasonable or threatening behaviour and obvious need to bypass the village is sufficient for the Council to fulfil its promise made so long ago to finish the last and most controversial final few hundred yards of tarmac. Is patience really a virtue?

Throughout the Middle Ages and until after the First World War, Winsley thrived as a self-contained rural community, its chief industries being agriculture, stone quarrying, stone masonry and, in earlier days, weaving. As weaving and quarrying died out an unexpected source of employment was provided for people both within and outside the parish with the arrival of the Chest Hospital.

Winsley Chest Hospital

At the end of the nineteenth century it was estimated that sixty thousand people yearly in England and Wales died from consumption, a form of tuberculosis, particularly within the poorer areas of towns and cities, where families were often crowded together in unventilated and unhygenic houses. There was nowhere locally where consumptives could be treated. In 1899 the 'Three Counties Branch' of the National Association for the Prevention of Tuberculosis was formed to organise a campaign covering Gloucestershire, Wiltshire and Somerset including Bristol. The outcome was a decision to finance and build a Sanatorium on a site at Winsley. Dr. Weatherly, Chairman of the Committee, was delighted:

> By all who are conversant with the needs as to site and situation of a sanatorium for consumptives, the land chosen by the Committee at Winsley has been thought to be ideal... Its sylvan scenery is very lovely. Murhill Quarry, in which the Sanatorium will be built, has a most beautiful outlook over the Wiltshire Downs with the White Horse at Westbury very distinctly visible... The Parish of Winsley has for generations been noted for its salubrity... The woods on the Estate are very pretty, and already lovely walks are practically made, and with much tree-planting on the land, there can be no doubt the surroundings of this Sanatorium will be hard to beat in this or any other country.

In December 1904 the hospital opened with sixteen patients and there were 180 admissions during the first year. Visiting experts of sanatoria arrived from

Germany and Switzerland, and Winsley Sanatorium was pronounced to be superior. Over the years the hospital provided treatment, rest and often cure for countless sufferers of the disease. By the 1920s it had become an outlying teaching centre for medical students from Bristol University and began to gain an international reputation. But by 1927 Pulmonary Tuberculosis was still the cause of at least forty thousand deaths a year in England and Wales and it was not until the late 1940s, when Streptomycin was discovered, that the death rate fell dramatically. Between 1904 and 1947 the total number of admissions to Winsley was 13,079. The following year, the hospital that had been financed by donations, legacies, scholarships, grants and the like, was administered by the Bath Hospital Management Committee, under the National Health System Act of 1946.

Winsley Chest Hospital in 1954.

By 1962 the decline in tuberculosis meant that half the hospital beds were occupied by non-tuberculosis patients. Admissions continued to decrease and by the 1970s a proportion of the beds were occupied by pre-convalescent patients. In 1975 the hospital was renamed 'Winsley Hospital' as chest cases diminished. The reorganization of health provision in the area saw the arrival of the Mental Handicap Unit in 1977 and the hospital was again renamed, this time as 'Winsley Centre'. Now only a small part of the hospital was being used to care for the mentally ill children and adolescents. The other buildings were falling into disrepair and in 1985 the Centre was closed as patients were housed in the community.

Over the years Winsley Hospital grew to become a showpiece of architecture, landscape gardening and woodland management. Gifts were showered on the patients and hospital alike. The active League of Friends, with branches in many nearby villages and towns, raised money for many of the amenities at the hospital, particularly the building of the Alexander Hall in 1955. Entertainers, from Welsh Choirs to BBC personalities, flocked to Winsley to provide enjoyment and fun for the patients and staff. The Autumn Fayre, which is sadly missed in Winsley, became an annual fund-raising event, always well attended by local people and invariably opened by a well-known personality. Jimmy Logan, John Doyle, Alan Taylor, Tom Salmon, Pearl Catlin, Godfrey Winn and Jan Leeming are just some of the people who supported Winsley but special mention should be made of Leslie Crowther who did so much to help the hospital, particularly when it became a Children's Mental Handicap Unit in 1977.

From 1985, when the Hospital was closed down, the buildings remained unused until a purchaser was found in 1988. The buildings had deteriorated rapidly and some have been demolished. However, the main buildings have been renovated carefully and sympathetically, the gardens are been reworked and in 1993 the hospital, now renamed Avon Park Care Centre, is once again open for business as a residential and nursing centre for the elderly.

Winsley House

To outsiders there is confusion as to where or what is Winsley House. The original house was built in 1637, its date still visible over its front door which is set in the wall of the main road which winds through the village. Above the door is one of three large stone dogs carved by a local mason many years ago. It was known as Winsley House Farm and remained a working farm until its demolition at the end of the nineteenth century. The lane opposite the door was once the farm lane which led past the barn (now Barn House) to the lane near the church. The farm pond was nearby, behind the Wheatsheaf.

In 1902 the present Winsley House was built some way back from the road. The cellars of the old farm connect underground with the new building. By the 1930s the house was owned by a Mr. and Mrs. Fowler. The daughter of their personal chauffeur, Irene Lintern, who still lives in the village, went with her family to live in part of the house in 1944. By then Mr. Fowler had died but his wife still lived in great style employing, besides a chauffeur, her own personal dresser, a cook, a butler and a parlourmaid. In 1953 Winsley House became vacant and was bought by the Governors of the Sutcliffe School in Bath, an organization which cared for maladjusted children. Until 1990 it was known as The Sutcliffe School. Diminishing numbers and financial difficulties led to its closure and sale in 1992 to the hospice movement known as Dorothy House and the building has been renamed Winsley House. If the huge cost of the planned extensive additions and alterations can be met by the public, the building, which enjoys the same magnificent situation and views as the adjacent Avon Park, will provide patients with a beautiful and superbly tranquil home.

Murhill

The lane which runs south on the west side of Winsley House used to be no more than a track with a stile and is still known by some as 'Rotten Gate'. It leads to the hamlet of Murhill, usually pronounced Murrell. It nestles in the warm seclusion of the wooded slopes with the valley laid out beneath it. It is a privilege to live in such a delectable place, as I do. Its interesting history is so well described in the *Winsley Village Scrapbook* by the late Mrs. Bridget Moorsom that, as a memorial to this long time resident and enthusiastic researcher of Winsley's past, her account of Murhill is included here.

The gardens of Murhill are much frequented by the gentry of Bath.' This, the earliest reference that has yet been found to Murhill, might have been made at anytime, for Murhill has long been famous for its strawberry gardens, but it does in fact come from a book in the time of Charles II, three hundred years ago, and refers perhaps, not to strawberry gardens but to 'pleasure gardens'; for in Murhill woods between Murhill Farm and Murhill House, there are very ancient yews, and the remains of steps and terraces which suggest that at one time the wood had been laid out as a garden.

On an old map dated about the middle of the 18th century, Murhill is not marked, but a house somewhere in these woods is shown as 'Mr. Cottle's House'. That there was a fairly large dwelling house here even earlier is also suggested by a list of Prominent Wiltshire Papists dated 1680 which includes the name of a Lady Banks. 'A Benedictine was chaplain to her at Murhill (Winsley) from sometime after 1700 until his death there in 1721.' (*The Victoria History of Wiltshire*, vol.III)

No trace of such a house now exists, nor has any tradition been handed down as to when or how it came to its end, but on a map dated probably between 1780 and 1800, no such house is shown but the present hamlet is shown under the name of 'Marvil'. (Elsewhere it is described as Murfield.) It is safe to conjecture therefore that some time between 1721 and 1789 the old house was destroyed and the new hamlet sprang up.

This new hamlet probably owed its existence to the opening up of the stone quarries in Murhill Cleeves and later, on the top of the hill, where the Winsley Chest Hospital now stands – 'Murhill stone' is a name known in the trade, at least locally. Exactly when these quarries were opened is not known, but they cannot have been greatly developed until the coming of the Kennet and Avon Canal, and the making of the 'trolley-way' which runs down the south side of the Murhill House garden and by which the blocks of stone were lowered to the wharf from which they were loaded into barges. The engine for the winding gear may have been housed in the old quarry in Murhill Cleeves, where until recently an old stone factory chimney stood, though others say this was a lime kiln.

The three 'ranks' of cottages which form the backbone of Murhill were probably built for quarrymen; it is certain that the present Murhill House was originally a rank of three cottages. Some time before 1841 this rank was converted into a house by building up the walls and putting on an upper story. In 1841 the house was further enlarged by adding on a wing at the west end, but the thatched roof was kept for another thirty years, when in 1873 the house was bought by Col. MacGrath who heightened the walls and put on a tiled roof....

The alterations to Murhill House in 1841 encorporated in the cellar the spring from which the house did, and still does, get its water supply. Springs are an important factor in life at Murhill. A series of them come out of the hillside round about the 300 ft. contour... Until 1914 all the houses east of Murhill House got their water from a pump depending on a spring just below the back gate to Murhill House but by 1914 the spring was drying up and the houses at the east end of Murhill 'went on the main'....The west end of Murhill has until very recently, been entirely dependant on springs for its water supply, but now a main has been laid down to this end of Murhill and houses have been connected with it.

On an enormous stone slab in the wall of the road to east Murhill is boldly carved 'In 1882 Colonel Magrath made this road'. This commemorates the fact that Colonel Magrath made that piece of road, having got permission of the Parish Council to alter the line of the old track which passed close behind the house. Murhill lane was metalled by public subscription by the people of Murhill and then taken over by the Rural District Council.

Forty years have passed since Mrs. Moorsom wrote about Murhill and very little has changed. Murhill House is still dependant on spring water and is still occupied by Lady Susan Marshall whose family have owned the house since the end of the last century. It is fascinating to descend the old cellar steps within

The Magrath Stone.

the house and gaze at the deep silent pool of water fed by the spring that has provided all the needs of the house for at least 150 years. Today the water is pumped up to a tank in the attic by an electric pump which automatically comes on when the tank is emptied. All other houses are supplied by the mains water.

Woodland now covers much of the hillside, but 150 years ago there were fewer trees and more cultivated land. The Tythe Map of 1841 lists William Stone Esq. as the owner of Winsley House and other property nearby. It also shows that he owned property in Murhill, listed as Garden/wood and gardens. The land shown on the map is a large rectangle below, and to the west of, the quarry and reaching down as far as a 'Common Coppice/wood' which bordered the canal. The area was mainly open space with a few trees at the top near the lane. Seen very clearly are curving pathways, obviously laid out as a garden, and there is a small entrance in the north west corner of the plot exactly where we find the old stone archway today. The garden would have been William Stone's pride and joy and he must have often walked down the lane from the village to visit it.

Later in the century the hillside was renowned for its productive fruit orchards which must have filled most of area where we find William Stone's garden. Until about fifty years ago strawberries were also grown in great quantities and sold commercially in London, having been loaded onto the train at Limpley Stoke. The strawberry gardens were famous and Murhill was a favourite place for walkers to stop and have a strawberry tea.

Canal Cottage, fruit orchards and the Kennet and Avon Canal below Murhill, 1892.

The face of the quarry is now hidden deep in the woods (on private property) although it is still possible but dangerous, and therefore not advisable, to find the entrance to the huge network of tunnels that spreads deep into the hillside. In the woods, beneath some magnificent beech trees, the tangled undergrowth covers some of the steps and walks that were created for the patients in the Sanatorium. There is still a single track through the wood which is delightful at any time of the year.

At the eastern end of the lane a narrow track leads either back into Winsley or down to Elbow Bridge and the canal towpath. From here a wider track takes the walker to Turleigh.

Turleigh (Turley)

Turleigh – a place of dignified houses and well-ordered cottages. Turleigh, with its attractive gardens, is charming at all times of the year. The warm corner in which is nestles seems to speak of peace and quietude. There is nothing to remind one of the busy turmoil of the modern world. Trees of every contrasting shade protect the houses, and in early summer, the blossom of many fruit trees adds to the scene. Later, when autumn begins to take on her barer outline, the contribution of dark-leaved evergreens becomes more noticeable. The village is well blessed by a cool and prolific water supply, Turleigh Troughs, which gushes generously out of the hillside, and which local legend claims has never gone dry. Turleigh was the birthplace of Sir Richard Atwood Glass, the constructor of the Atlantic Telegraph Cable. (Lewis E. Brown: *In and Around the Limpley Stoke Valley*, 1947.)

Lewis Brown's description fits Turleigh as well today as it did forty-seven years ago. The Conservation Area encompasses the whole of the village. Every building in Turleigh is constructed of stone, either random rubble, coursed rubble or coursed ashlar. Many are from the seventeenth and eighteenth centuries including Uplands House and Turleigh Farmhouse. The ghosts of Turleigh's recent history cannot be avoided when walking through the village. 'The Old Post Office', 'The Old Malt House', 'The Old Tannery', are inscribed above doorways and on walls as one passes the old chapel and the rank of cottages that used to be the pub named the Prince of Wales. Yet this village, that has lost many of its amenities, retains its character in its lovely architecture, its beautiful gardens and trees and its ancient water supply. The Turleigh Trows, a series of seven roughly sculpted stone troughs, clothed in lichen and moss and shaded by an enormous beech tree, are filled by a conduit from some distance up the hill. The water flows on under the road and fills the mill pond in the garden near the old mill.

The mill, which used to be two weavers' houses, is now a private house with a garden set in terraces leading down to the mill pond. The mill was used to grinding bark for tanning and dates back to 1600 A.D. Beyond the mill and in a dip in the road to Bradford is the Old Malt House, a brewery at the beginning of the century and restored from its ruinous state as a coal yard without a roof about fifty years ago.

Turleigh House was built in the middle of the sixteenth century, added to in the seventeenth century, and almost entirely rebuilt early in the eighteenth century (VHCW). Recently, local people have watched in awe as the building, its grounds and the adjacent chapel, c.1800, have undergone extensive restoration. Tantalizing glimpses of water gardens, fountains, a gazebo, terraces, stone walling and extensive tree and shrub planting can just be seen over the high walls. One is reminded of the eighteenth century when landscape gardeners were given a free hand to sculpt and beautify the English countryside. It is good to think it can still happen in the twentieth century.

Turleigh House.

The fortunate past residents of Turleigh House have included Sir Richard Atwood who, as a wealthy Bradford clothier, moved to Turleigh at the end of the eighteenth century. He bought the freehold of the house together with some 373 acres of farm land in Winsley, Holt and Bradford Leigh. He died in 1808 but his widow, Ann Atwood, lived until 1842 when she was ninety-two. So generous was she with her wealth that she became known as Lady Bountiful. She largely financed the rebuilding of Winsley Church and gave alms freely for the poor. Included in the *Winsley Scrapbook* of 1954 is an essay by schoolgirl Muriel Hayter on 'Turley Baptist Chapel':

> This chapel is at the present time unused, and has been for about forty five years; but formerly it was built by the owner of Turley House, as a place of worship for the village people....I have been able to go back as far as when Lady Attwood lived at Turley House.

It is said that when all the congregation had arrived at the chapel, her ladyship would enter, followed by her butler carrying a prayer book on a velvet cushion. Then everyone stood, while she went to her private pew; then when she was seated, she motioned them to sit down. The service then proceeded as usual, to the end, when all the people remained in their seats till Lady Attwood had left the chapel....It is known by some of the older inhabitants of Turley and Winsley that often the chapel would be crowded and a long queue waiting, which reached nearly as far as Mr. Elliot's shop, on a fine Sunday evening.

When this kind person died, she left a certain amount of money to be given to charity, each year, for the Winsley Parish, and this is still carried on.

A footnote in the *Scrapbook* reads:

Muriel's Father, the Rev. W. Hayter, was the Evangelist of the Trowbridge Wesleyan Circuit for 42 years. He lived in Turleigh and was much beloved by his flock, being a good and kindly man. He was particularly kind to the old and sick folk, and used regularly to visit them in the hospital and workhouse. He gained the confidence and affection of the gypsies in the neighbourhood, and at the yearly Fair at Bradford Leigh, the gypsies would bring their babies and he would baptise them in a part of the fairground set apart for this purpose. He died in 1939.

Conkwell

Beyond the weir at Limpley Stoke the Avon flows northwards and for the next couple of miles the eastern slopes of the valley are clothed with an unbroken ridge of trees except for one small breach. Conkwell, with its cluster of Cotswold stone houses, seems to be pushing its way out of the woods that enfold it. This mysterious little place dates back to prehistoric times, but its more recent history includes an eighteenth century trolley-way to carry stone from its quarry to Dundas, a wishing-well of some repute, a steep lane to nowhere that cars would do best to avoid, and a favourite home of the present Governor of Hong Kong.

Conkwell and Warleigh Woods are divided by the lane and, seen from the southern slopes, the different shades of green in summer and the blaze of colour as the trees rust into autumn, particularly the gold of the larches, are one of the finest sights in the valley. Yet in 1969 all was not well in Conkwell Woods.

In the summer of that year Sir Eric Milbourn of Conkwell Grange 'clear-felled' twelve acres of woodland on the slopes near Conkwell and incurred the wrath of the people on the other side of the valley. With headlines such as HOW GREEN WAS MY VALLEY and WHY I AXED MY TREES, BY SIR ERIC the local press kept the story in the public eye for some time. The woods were owned by Sir Eric and partly controlled by the Forestry Commission who had approved his action to fell. It is interesting, nearly twenty-five years later, to read comments made at the time and look today at the hillside after replanting.

A public meeting was held in Limpley Stoke. Sir Eric maintained that he was trying to beautify the valley for future generations. Villagers complained of the terrible scar left by the felling of mature hardwood trees and replacing them with rows of larch. The man from the Forestry Commission explained that beech trees had also been planted and that the elm would regenerate. 'They would not, as feared, all grow in straight lines', he said. 'The scar will have gone by this time next year. The new trees will have covered the ground in five year's time and thinning will have broken up the straight lines in 15 years'. The County Council's assistant clerk said, 'It should be appreciated that trees are a crop as well as an amenity. It is no good leaving them until they are too old and rotten to be of any use before felling.'

The meeting was not convinced and continued to mourn the loss of the hardwood trees. They passed a resolution asking Somerset and Wiltshire County Councils to hire a landscape architect to look at the whole valley and advise them on its future. This was duly done and in 1970 Sylvia Crowe, CBE, PPILA, delivered her *Landscape Report on Woodlands in the Limpley Stoke Valley*. She hoped that a detailed landscape survey 'could provide a basis for enlisting the co-operation of landowners, local authorities and amenity societies'. She also felt that:

> In my opinion, the objections to the clear felling in Conkwell Wood have been due less to the extent of the felling than to its shape and to the very strongly marked stripes at its lower edge.
>
> The rectangle taken out contradicts the characteristic shapes of the valley landscape. These shapes are varied and tend to take a diagonal line across the contours, rarely a vertical or horizontal one.

She went on to suggest the type of tree to be planted and various ways and means of shaping the landscape by felling according to the formation of the ground, leaving promontories of timber standing on the knolls. Even to the uniniatiated it is a revealing and interesting document to read. It is the Forestry Commission who have effective control over the trees in the valley and these policies, if they have been taken into account, should provide for the future. Privatising the Forestry Commission would not seem to be a good idea.

The hillside in 1993 may not please everyone and does show signs of the twelve acres having been clear felled, but for those who did not know the wood before 1969 it is lovely to look on. The early flush of green of the larches in the spring and splash of gold in the autumn is a wonderful sight. True the elms never regenerated but they would have died anyway. The hillside is still intact and lessons have been learned.

At the time the clear felling was taking place another, more permanent eyesore, was being suggested. In 1969 BBC Television reception in the valley was poor. To provide both BBC television channels effectively, it was proposed that a 185 foot television transmitting mast should be sited on the ridge at Conkwell. A few people objected to these proposals but were shouted down by the television watchers. One viewer from Freshford wrote to the local paper to say she liked the idea of 'a tall slender mast, rising like a silver spire above the trees'. In March of that year the Bradford and Melksham Rural District Council gave the idea its blessing, first having been greatly concerned by the threat to trees and the beauty of the valley, but being reassurred by the BBC engineering department. Only one man, Sir Hugo Marshall, remained totally unconvinced and voted against the acceptance of the transmitter.

Eventually, Wiltshire County Council refused permission. Happily the trees have regenerated but now, in 1994, Conkwell and the valley are fighting another transmitter proposal. This time it is not to be a slender spire but an ugly hundred-foot high tower, ten foot across at the top – its narrowest point. District Council policy on transmitter towers states that they are acceptable 'unless there are problems.' At the time of writing the Planning Committee has yet to make up its mind as to whether this inevitable eyesore in an AONB is a 'problem'.

Westwood

The village of Westwood is found one mile to the south-west of Bradford on Avon. From its vantage point high on the hill at the western extremity of Wiltshire, Upper and Lower Westwood have an almost panoramic view of the surrounding countryside. Far-reaching views over the fertile fields of Somerset stretch to the south and east, and to the north and west are the wooded valleys of the Avon and Frome. The hamlet of Avoncliff straddles the river at the bottom of the steep slopes to the north. Iford with Staples Hill lie to the west, close to the county borders of Avon and Somerset. These hamlets, with the village, comprise the parish of Westwood.

Much of the land to the north and east, including the two river valleys, are designated an area of High Ecological Value. Areas of Conservation cover Lower Westwood, Avoncliff and Upper Westwood – that part of Westwood, including the stone quarry, which stands on the ridge overlooking the Avon Valley. The heart of the village, known as Westwood, is covered by the Village Policy Limit which allows limited development with certain restrictions. The whole parish is covered by Green Belt.

Within the boundaries of the parish are found two of England's delightful small country houses, both dating back to the Middle Ages – Westwood Manor, now owned by the National Trust, and Iford Manor on the River Frome. The house and garden at Westwood are open to the public, as is the unique Italianate garden at Iford. Both are magnificent settings for outdoor plays and music. Iford's 1993 week-long festival of entertainment, including a Jazz concert and a Restoration play performed in the Cloisters, is of the highest standard. All who attended these and the growing number of similar performances in villages close by find a wealth of talent, both musical and dramatic.

Although there is some evidence of prehistoric and Roman occupation around Westwood, recorded history dates from 983 A.D. when the Saxon King Ethelred granted various large tracts of land close to the modern village, first to his servant Aelfnoth and, four years later, to his huntsman Leofwine. After the Norman Conquest, Domesday records that Westwood was in the possession of the Priory of Winchester. Thereafter, the ownership of Westwood is somewhat confused. Although it was nominally part of the Bradford Hundred until the sixteenth century, it had at some earlier date become part of the Hundred of Everleigh and Elstub which paid allegiance to Winchester Priory (VCHW Vol XI). The histories of the manor and the church diverged in the thirteenth century and the church at Westwood was made part of the Parish of Bradford on Avon. In 1982 the parishes of Westwood and Wingfield joined together and at present share a rector. However, under new proposals now being considered, the villages could lose their rector due to lack of clergy and funds.

Westwood Manor and Church.

For centuries the small agricultural settlement at Lower Westwood and its associated corn and fulling mills at Avoncliff and Iford, and perhaps a small settlement at Upper Westwood, supported a population of about sixty or seventy people. In time the cloth trade and stone quarries boosted the numbers and at Avoncliff in the 1770s a group of weavers' cottages was built, known today as Anciff Square. During the depression in the 1800s the building became the local workhouse and at one time increased the population of Westwood by at least two hundred people. Today the village population is around fourteen hundred.

Westwood Manor

The changing economic situation in the sixteenth century, brought about by the burgeoning cloth trade in the district, enabled clothiers to amass large fortunes which they invested in the purchase and improvement of property. This money also provided for the building and embellishment of churches. Westwood is a prime example of manor house and church benefitting from the personal fortune of one family.

Thomas Horton, a leading clothier in the district, and already a wealthy man, acquired the lease on Westwood in 1518 and set about the alteration and enlargement of the few small buildings which were already there. The Dining Room, its exquisite moulded oak rib ceiling, the Panelled Room above, the lovely oriel window and the Gothic Room all date from the sixteenth century, during almost one hundred years of occupation by the Horton family. Besides his other considerable building ventures in Bradford on Avon and elsewhere, Thomas Horton's benefactions to Westwood Church were considerable. The Lady Chapel, the tower and the Priest's House (now demolished) were legacies of his wealth and interest in buildings. The Manor House, together with its tithe barn and the adjacent church provide a delightful architectural picture.

The seventeenth century saw a change in ownership to John Farewell. He lived in Westwood Manor from 1616 and the monument in the church records his death in 1642. His widow continued to live at the Manor until 1674. As fast as he demolished parts of the old building, Farewell made many improvements. He had inherited a small agricultural estate and he set about transforming the house that was at its centre. He demolished the north and west rear wings and probably the long south-east wing, erecting in its place a wing at the east corner (demolished in about 1860). He built the turret staircase and the present porch and he remodelled much of the interior of the house, converting the top part of the Great Hall into a delightful room known as the Great Parlour.

In 1649 a survey of the house made by the Commonwealth Commissioners for the sale of church lands, described the estate as:

> all that capital messuage called the farm house of the manor of Westwood, consisting of a hall, a parlour wainscotted, a kitchen, a buttery, a dairy-house, a brew house, six lodging chambers, two garretts, a stable, a barn, an ox-stall, a cow-stall, a wain-house, a sheep-house, a hay house, a garden, an orchard, a dovehouse reasonably well stored and a yard, worth per annum £5.
>
> *(Westwood Manor: National Trust)*

During Georgian times, when new architectural styles were being introduced in Bradford on Avon and Bath, Westwood Manor went into something of a decline. It was increasingly seen to be old-fashioned and was spurned by the smart, well-to-do families of the eighteenth century. But fashions come and go, and by the nineteenth century its architectural merits were again admired and became the subject of artists such as John Skinner and J.C. Buckler. Their drawings of the Manor are in the British Museum.

Rescued from its use as a mere farmhouse, its central range of buildings covered in ivy, Westwood Manor was sold in 1911 to E.G. Lister who set about its renovation 'with fine taste, making a number of sensible and restrained restorations'. Besides his noble aims for the renovation of the Manor, Lister's two other passions were needlework and music and he enhanced the interior of the house with the display of early musical instruments and fine patterned needlework coverings on the furniture. Both are set against a background of superb oak furniture, oak-panelled rooms and exquisite plasterwork.

In 1943 Mr. Lister provided protective covenants over the Manor for the National Trust who took over its ownership, along with the furniture and endowment, after his death in 1956. The Trust inherited a house structurally unchanged since the 1650s, an unpretentious two-storey building set in a garden filled with topiary and a large pond. At first glance the Manor has a modest aspect which belies its long and interesting history. It has had an unbroken succession of inhabitants since the fifteenth century. From that time, and particularly in the sixteenth century, it was extended from the original small structure, probably built around 1400 AD, to the mellowing, exquisite Manor House that visitors see today.

During the Second World War the stone quarries became a war equipment factory and storage space for valuables – even providing a hangar for the aeroplane used by Bleriot to cross the channel in 1909. Workers, who were brought from the Midlands, were employed there to build the famous Enfield Motor Cycle. They were housed in ninety-four bungalows built by the War Department. Acquired by the Council in 1960, this temporary accommodation eventually became the nucleus of the new estate at Westwood, with its primary school, Post Office and village store. The centre of the village, for so long found near the church, Manor House and inn, thus became relocated in the new estate.

Westwood Mine

Westwood stone mine originally opened as a source of stone for the building of the Great Western Railway. Miners with picks and saws carved a labyrinth of tunnels, eight-feet high and twelve feet wide, under Westwood with the help of candles and oil lamps. It was shut down in 1920 due to falling prices and was used to grow mushrooms, favoured by its constant temperature of fifty degrees Fahrenheit, until a disease infected them in 1937. In 1970 the mine was reopened and continues to produce huge honey-coloured limestone blocks used in such buildings as the new Bradford on Avon Library.

Avoncliff

The Westwood quarry tramway was opened in 1877 to transport stone from the mine to the railway siding at Avoncliff in the valley below. Its squat trolleys ran on the two-foot-five-inch gauge via a double tracked incline. The loaded trolley descended at the end of a rope and pulled empty trolleys up the other track. It descended the hill beside paths that had connected Upper Westwood with Avoncliff for centuries and where the two grist and fulling mills had stood for so long, one each side of the Avon.

The mill on the Westwood side of the Avon was bought in 1700 by William Chandler when it was still a corn mill. By 1731 it was still grinding corn but had a bakehouse attached and was also used as a dye-house. In 1763 it was converted into a fulling mill and in 1781 it was sold to the Yerbury family. It was during their ownership that a boy of twelve who was employed at the mill became trapped in the machinery and died. The rather gruesome inquest provided evidence of some of the earliest machinery in a mill at that time. After various tenancies and owners the factory was converted into a flock mill in 1860. When the owner, J A Wheeler, offered it for sale in 1878 it included a main mill, a south mill, two stove houses and power supplied by a turbine wheel and a pressure steam engine. It remained as a flock mill until the Second World War. The main mill still stands and so does the south mill which has been converted into a house. Above them towers the old brick chimney stack.

On the Bradford side of the river are the delapidated rusting remains of another flock mill, its large iron wheel with paddles still in position. In the sixteenth century the building was described as being a grist and fulling mill under one roof but in the eighteenth century the property was divided. The grist mill was sold separately and was eventually demolished, probably when the railway was built. The fulling mill was sold to Francis Yerbury in 1740 and it appears his son, William Yerbury, occupied the mill and continued there until about 1811. In 1880 T R Freeman of Monkton Combe used it in the flock business and was followed by William Selwyn who ran both the mills at Avoncliff until the Second World War.

This section of the canal between Bradford and Limpley Stoke, particularly at Avoncliff, has been notorious for land slippage producing water loss. This has necessitated the art of 'puddling' – filling the cracks in the canal bed with clay. The clay has been extracted from a clay pit known as Gripwood Quarry, found close to the canal south of the Tithe Barn. (The quarry is now designated a Site of Special Scientific Interest.) Recently, more serious landslips have taken place in this area and the canal was drained for major renovation. It has now been rebuilt and lined with reinforced concrete and is open again for an ever-increasing boating population.

To many, the sights and sounds of Avoncliff constitute the heart of the Limpley

Stoke Valley. Its two mills, one renovated as a dwelling and the other in a state of pleasing decay, standing either side of the pounding water of the weir with its curiously evocative smell, point to a history of industry and wealth. The mills and the river are encompassed by the snaking forms of the railway and the canal. Rennie's magnificent aqueduct, which carries the canal high above the river and railway, strides across the gorge from one steep, wooded hillside to the other. Below the seventeenth century Cross Guns Inn stands a lone weeping willow, its roots almost permanently washed by the Avon. Each year the greening of this willow heralds the coming of spring to the valley. As the winter floods recede from the foot of the tree the barges, with their attractive canal motifs, moor alongside the canal wharf, many bedecked with plants and flowers, to enjoy another season in this beautiful valley.

The Avon in full flood at Avoncliff.

Bibliography

Allsopp, Niall: *The Kennet and Avon Canal*, 1987
Allsopp, Niall: *The Somersetshire Coal Canal*, 1993
Aston, M & Burrow, I (eds.): *The Archaeology of Somerset*, 1982
Aston, M & Iles, R (eds.): *The Archaeology of Avon*
Barron, R S: *The Geology of Wiltshire: a Field Guide*, 1976
Bettey, J: *Wessex from AD 1000*, 1986
Claverton Women's Institute: *A History of Claverton*, 1956
Clew, Kenneth: *The Kennet and Avon Canal*, 1968
Collinson, Rev. John: *A History of Antiquities in the County of Somerset*, 1791
Cunliffe, B: *The City of Bath*, 1986
Cunliffe, B: *Roman Bath Discovered*, 1971
Fassnidge, Harold: *Bradford on Avon Past and Present*, 1993
Gillham, B: *The Wiltshire Flora*, 1993
Grose, D: *Flora of Wiltshire*, 1989
Hamilton, M: *Bath before Beau Nash*, 1978
Hooker, R.: *Limpley Stoke from Roman Times to the Present Day*
Jefferies, Richard: *Wild Life in a Southern County*, reprinted 1978
Jones, Roger: *Down the Bristol Avon*, 1983
Jones, Rev. W H & Jackson, E: *Bradford on Avon*, 1907
Kennet & Avon Canal Trust: *Claverton Pumping Station*, 1984
Langdon, Gee: *The Year of the Map*, 1976
Laurence, G L: *Bathford Past and Present*, 1985
Pevsner, N: *North Somerset and Bristol*, 1958
Pitcairn, Rev. D. Lee & Richardson, Rev. A.: *A Historical Guide to Monkton Combe, Combe Down and Claverton.*
Ponting, K G: *Wool and Water*, 1975
Powell, W R: *Bradford on Avon: A History to 1950* – offprint from VHCS.
Rogers, K H: *Wiltshire and Somerset Woollen Mills*, 1976
Sharkey, John: *Celtic Mysteries*, 1975
Slocombe, P: *Wiltshire Farm Buildings 1500-1900*, 1989
Tanner, R & H: *Woodland Plants*, 1981
Terson, Peter: *Under the Fish and Over the Water*, 1990
Trevelyan, G M: *A Shortened History of England*, 1942
Tucker, D E: *The Bristol Avon*, 1987
Walls, Ernest: *The Bristol Avon*, 1927
Waugh, Ken & Margaret: *A Glimpse of Bathford the Walled Village*, 1982
Whitlock, Ralph: *Wildlife in Wessex*, 1976
Willett, John: *Hospital Diary: the History of Winsley Chest Hospital*, 1993
Wroughton, Dr. J: *The Perfect Chronicler – The Battle of Lansdown*, 1993

Papers, Booklets and Leaflets:
Avon Wildlife Trust Booklets
Barton Farm Country Park booklet
Crowe, Sylvia: Landscape Report on Woodlands in the Limpley Stoke Valley.
Limpley Stoke Hydro Brochure, 1892
Church leaflets: St. Mary's, Limpley Stoke; Westwood.
Dept. of the Environment: *Farleigh Hungerford Castle* – Official Guide
Dodge, Dr. A: *Freshford Church*
Fox, Lady: 'Wansdyke Reconsidered'; Archael. Journal, Vol. 115, 1958
Perkins, J W et al: *Bath Stone*
Stone, J F & Wicks, A T: *Archaeological finds at Hayes Wood, Freshford*, (SANHS vol 81, 1935)
Wainwright, G J: *An Iron Age Promontory Fort at Budbury, Bradford on Avon*, (WANHS vol 65, 1970)
West Wiltshire District Plan for deposit: West Wiltshire District Council, 1993
Williams, W J & Stoddart, D M: *Bath – Some Encounters with Science*, 1978
Wiltshire Trust for Nature Conservation: Ancient Woodlands of Wiltshire

INDEX

Page references in bold type refer to chapters or chapter sub-sections; those in italic type refer to illustrations. Some listings, such as churches and pubs, are grouped under an appropriate heading.